# Stories by Foreign Authors: Polish

*Various*

# Contents

# STORIES BY FOREIGN AUTHORS: POLISH

BY

Various

# THE LIGHT-HOUSE KEEPER OF ASPINWALL
## BY
## HENRYK SIENKIEWICZ

## CHAPTER I

On a time it happened that the light-house keeper in Aspinwall, not far from Panama, disappeared without a trace. Since he disappeared during a storm, it was supposed that the ill-fated man went to the very edge of the small, rocky island on which the light-house stood, and was swept out by a wave. This supposition seemed the more likely as his boat was not found next day in its rocky niche. The place of light-house keeper had become vacant. It was necessary to fill this place at the earliest moment possible, since the light-house had no small significance for the local movement as well as for vessels going from New York to Panama. Mosquito Bay abounds in sandbars and banks. Among these navigation, even in the daytime, is difficult; but at night, especially with the fogs which are so frequent on those waters warmed by the sun of the tropics, it is nearly impossible. The only guide at that time for the numerous vessels is the light-house.

The task of finding a new keeper fell to the United States consul living in Panama, and this task was no small one: first, because it was absolutely necessary to find the man within twelve hours; second, the man must be unusually conscientious,--it was not possible, of course, to take the first comer at random; finally, there was an utter lack of candidates. Life on a tower is uncommonly difficult, and by no means enticing to people of the South, who love idleness and the freedom of a vagrant life. That light-house keeper is almost a prisoner. He cannot leave his rocky island except on Sundays. A boat from Aspinwall brings him provisions and water once a day, and returns immediately; on the whole island, one acre in area, there is no inhabitant. The keeper lives in the light-house; he keeps it in order. During the day he gives signals by displaying flags of various colors to indicate changes of the barometer; in the evening he lights the lantern. This would be no great labor were it not that to reach the lantern at the summit of the tower he must pass over more than four hundred steep and very high steps; sometimes he must make this journey repeatedly during the day. In general, it is the life of a monk, and indeed more than that,--the life of a hermit. It was not wonderful, therefore, that Mr. Isaac Falconbridge was in no small anxiety as to where he should find a permanent successor to the recent keeper; and it is easy to understand his joy when a successor announced himself most unexpectedly on that very day. He was a man already old, seventy years or more, but fresh, erect, with the movements and bearing of a soldier. His hair was perfectly white, his face as dark as that of a Creole; but, judging from his blue eyes, he did not belong to a people of the South. His face was somewhat downcast and sad, but honest. At the first glance he pleased Falconbridge. It remained only to examine him. Therefore the following conversation began:

"Where are you from?"

"I am a Pole."

"Where have you worked up to this time?"

"In one place and another."

"A light-house keeper should like to stay in one place."

"I need rest."

"Have you served? Have you testimonials of honorable government service?"

The old man drew from his bosom a piece of faded silk resembling a strip of an old flag, unwound it, and said:

"Here are the testimonials. I received this cross in 1830. This second one is Spanish from the Carlist War; the third is the French legion; the fourth I received in Hungary. Afterward I fought in the States against the South; there they do not give crosses."

Falconbridge took the paper and began to read.

"H'm! Skavinski? Is that your name? H'm! Two flags captured in a bayonet attack. You were a gallant soldier."

"I am able to be a conscientious light-house keeper."

"It is necessary to ascend the tower a number of times daily. Have you sound legs?"

"I crossed the plains on foot." (The immense steppes between the East and California are called "the plains.")

"Do you know sea service?"

"I served three years on a whaler."

"You have tried various occupations."

"The only one I have not known is quiet."

"Why is that?"

The old man shrugged his shoulders. "Such is my fate."

"Still you seem to me too old for a light-house keeper."

"Sir," exclaimed the candidate suddenly in a voice of emotion, "I am greatly wearied, knocked about. I have passed through much as you see. This place is one of those which I have wished for most ardently. I am old, I need rest. I need to say to myself, 'Here you will remain; this is your port.' Ah, sir, this depends now on you alone. Another time perhaps such a place will not offer itself. What luck that I was in Panama! I entreat you--as God is dear to me, I am like a ship which if it misses the harbor will be lost. If you wish to make an old man happy- -I swear to you that I am honest, but--I have enough of wandering."

The blue eyes of the old man expressed such earnest entreaty that Falconbridge, who had a good, simple heart, was touched.

"Well," said he, "I take you. You are light-house keeper."

The old man's face gleamed with inexpressible joy.

"I thank you."

"Can you go to the tower to-day?"

"I can."

"Then good-bye. Another word,--for any failure in service you will be dismissed."

"All right."

That same evening, when the sun had descended on the other side of the isthmus, and a day of sunshine was followed by a night without twilight, the new keeper was in his place evidently, for the light-house was casting its bright rays on the water as usual. The night was perfectly calm, silent, genuinely tropical, filled with a transparent haze, forming around the moon a great colored rainbow with soft, unbroken edges; the sea was moving only because the tide raised it. Skavinski on the balcony seemed from below like a small black point. He tried to collect his thoughts and take in his new position; but his mind was too much under pressure to move with regularity. He felt somewhat as a hunted beast feels when at last it has found refuge from pursuit on some inaccessible rock or in a cave. There had come to him, finally, an hour of quiet; the feeling of safety filled his soul with a certain unspeakable bliss. Now on that rock he can simply laugh at his previous wanderings, his misfortunes and failures. He was in truth like a ship whose masts, ropes, and sails had been broken and rent by a tempest, and cast from the clouds to the bottom of the sea,--a ship on which the tempest had hurled waves and spat foam, but which still wound its way to the harbor. The pictures of that storm passed quickly through his mind as he compared it with the calm future now beginning. A part of his wonderful adventures he had related to Falconbridge; he had not mentioned, however, thousands of other incidents. It had been his misfortune that as often as he pitched his tent and fixed his fireplace to settle down permanently, some wind tore out the stakes of his tent, whirled away the fire, and bore him on toward destruction. Looking now from the balcony of the tower at the illuminated waves, he remembered everything through which he had passed. He had campaigned in the four parts of the world, and in wandering had tried almost every occupation. Labor-loving and honest, more than once had he earned money, and had always lost it in spite of every prevision and the utmost caution. He had been a gold-miner in Australia, a diamond-digger in Africa, a rifleman in public service in the East Indies. He established a ranch in California,--the drought ruined him; he tried trading with wild tribes in the interior of Brazil,--his raft was wrecked on the Amazon; he himself alone, weaponless, and nearly naked, wandered in the forest for many weeks living on wild fruits, exposed every moment to death from the jaws of wild beasts. He established a forge in Helena, Arkansas, and that was burned in a great fire which consumed the whole town. Next he fell into the hands of Indians in the Rocky Mountains, and only through a miracle was he saved by Canadian trappers. Then he served as a sailor on a vessel running between Bahia and Bordeaux, and as harpooner on a whaling-ship; both vessels were wrecked. He had a cigar factory in Havana, and was robbed by his partner while he himself was lying sick with the vomito. At last he came to Aspinwall, and there was to be the end of his failures,-- for what could reach him on that rocky island? Neither water nor fire nor men. But from men Skavinski had not suffered much; he had met good men oftener than bad ones.

But it seemed to him that all the four elements were persecuting him. Those who knew him said that he had no luck, and with that they explained everything. He himself became somewhat of a monomaniac. He believed that some mighty and vengeful hand was pursuing him everywhere, on all lands and waters. He did not like, however, to speak of this; only at times, when some one asked him whose hand that could be, he pointed mysteriously to the Polar Star, and said, "It comes from that place." In reality his failures were so continuous that they were wonderful, and might easily drive a nail into the head, especially of the man who had experienced them. But Skavinski had the patience of an Indian, and that great calm power of resistance which comes from truth of heart. In his time he had received in Hungary a number of bayonet- thrusts because he would not grasp at a stirrup which was shown as means of salvation to him, and cry for quarter. In like manner he did not bend to misfortune. He crept up against the mountain as industriously as an ant. Pushed down a hundred times, he began his journey calmly for the hundred and first time. He was in his way a most peculiar original. This old soldier, tempered, God knows in how many fires, hardened in suffering, hammered and forged, had the heart of a child. In the time of the epidemic in Cuba, the vomito attacked him because he had given to the sick all his quinine, of which he had a considerable supply, and left not a grain to himself.

There had been in him also this wonderful quality,--that after so many disappointments he was ever full of confidence, and did not lose hope that all would be well yet. In winter he grew lively, and predicted great events. He waited for these events with impatience, and lived with the thought of them whole summers. But the winters passed one after another, and Skavinski lived only to this,--that they whitened his head. At last he grew old, began to lose energy; his endurance was becoming more and more like resignation, his former calmness was tending toward supersensitiveness, and that tempered soldier was degenerating into a man ready to shed tears for any cause. Besides this, from time to time he was weighed down by a terrible homesickness which was roused by any circumstance,--the sight of swallows, gray birds like sparrows, snow on the mountains, or melancholy music like that heard on a time. Finally, there was one idea which mastered him,--the idea of rest. It mastered the old man thoroughly, and swallowed all other desires and hopes. This ceaseless wanderer could not imagine anything more to be longed for, anything more precious, than a quiet corner in which to rest, and wait in silence for the end. Perhaps specially because some whim of fate had so hurried him over all seas and lands that he could hardly catch his breath, did he imagine that the highest human happiness was simply not to wander. It is true that such modest happiness was his due; but he was so accustomed to disappointments that he thought of rest as people in general think of something which is beyond reach. He did not dare to hope for it. Meanwhile, unexpectedly, in the course of twelve hours he had gained a position which was as if chosen for him out of all the world. We are not to wonder, then, that when he lighted his lantern in the evening he became as it were dazed,--that he asked himself if that was reality, and he did not dare to answer that it was. But at the same time reality convinced him with incontrovertible proofs; hence hours one after another passed while he was on the balcony. He gazed, and convinced himself. It might seem that he was looking at the sea for the first time in his life. The lens of the lantern cast into the darkness an enormous triangle of light, beyond which the eye of the old man was lost in the black distance completely, in the distance mysterious and awful. But that distance seemed to run toward the light. The long waves following one another rolled out from the darkness, and went bellowing toward the base of the island; and then their foaming backs were visible, shining rose-colored in the light of the lantern. The incoming tide swelled more and more, and covered the sandy bars. The mysterious speech of the ocean came with a fulness more powerful and louder, at one time like the thunder of cannon, at another like the roar of great forests, at another like the distant dull sound of the voices of people. At moments it was quiet; then to the ears of the old man came some great sigh, then a kind of sobbing, and again threatening outbursts. At last the wind bore away the haze, but brought black, broken clouds, which hid the moon. From the west it began to blow more and more; the waves sprang with rage against the rock of the light-house, licking with foam the foundation walls. In the distance a storm was beginning to bellow. On the dark, disturbed expanse certain green lanterns gleamed from the masts of ships. These green points rose high and then sank; now they swayed to the right, and now to the left. Skavinski descended to his room. The storm began to howl. Outside, people on those ships were struggling with night, with darkness, with waves; but inside the tower it was calm and still. Even the sounds of the storm hardly came through the thick walls, and only the measured tick-tack of the clock lulled the wearied old man to his slumber.

# CHAPTER II.

Hours, days, and weeks began to pass. Sailors assert that sometimes when the sea is greatly roused, something from out the midst of night and darkness calls them by name. If the infinity of the sea may call out thus, perhaps when a man is growing old, calls come to him, too, from another infinity still darker and more deeply mysterious; and the more he is wearied by life the dearer are those calls to him. But to hear them quiet is needed. Besides old age loves to put itself aside as if with a foreboding of the grave. The light-house had become for Skavinski such a half grave. Nothing is more monotonous than life on a beacon- tower. If young people consent to take up this service they leave it after a time. Light-house keepers are generally men not young, gloomy, and confined to themselves. If by chance one of them leaves his light- house and goes among men, he walks in the midst of them like a person roused from deep slumber. On the tower there is a lack of minute impressions which in ordinary life teach men to adapt themselves to everything. All that a light-house keeper comes in contact with is gigantic, and devoid of definitely outlined forms. The sky is one whole, the water another; and between those two infinities the soul of man is in loneliness. That is a life in which thought is continual meditation, and out of that meditation nothing rouses the keeper, not even his work. Day is like day as two beads in a rosary, unless changes of weather form the only variety. But Skavinski felt more happiness than ever in life before. He rose with the dawn, took his breakfast, polished the lens, and then sitting on the balcony gazed into the distance of the water; and his eyes were never sated with the pictures which he saw before him. On the enormous turquoise ground of the ocean were to be seen generally flocks of swollen sails gleaming in the rays of the sun so brightly that the eyes were blinking before the excess of light. Sometimes the ships, favored by the so-called trade winds, went in an extended line one after another, like a chain of sea-mews or albatrosses. The red casks indicating the channel swayed on the light wave with gentle movement. Among the sails appeared every afternoon gigantic grayish feather-like plumes of smoke. That was a steamer from New York which brought passengers and goods to Aspinwall, drawing behind it a frothy path of foam. On the other side of the balcony Skavinski saw, as if on his palm, Aspinwall and its busy harbor, and in it a forest of masts, boats, and craft; a little farther, white houses and the towers of the town. From the height of his tower the small houses were like the nests of sea- mews, the boats were like beetles, and the people moved around like small points on the white stone boulevard. From early morning a light eastern breeze brought a confused hum of human life, above which predominated the whistle of steamers. In the afternoon six o'clock came; the movement in the harbor began to cease; the mews hid themselves in the rents of the cliffs; the waves grew feeble and became in some sort lazy; and then on the land, on the sea, and on the tower came a time of stillness unbroken by anything. The yellow sands from which the waves had fallen back glittered like golden stripes on the width of the waters; the body of the tower was outlined definitely in blue. Floods of sunbeams were poured from the sky on the water and the sands and the cliff. At that time a certain lassitude full of sweetness seized the old man. He felt that the rest which he was enjoying was excellent; and when he thought that it would be continuous nothing was lacking to him.

Skavinski was intoxicated with his own happiness; and since a man adapts himself easily to improved conditions, he gained faith and confidence by degrees; for he thought that if men built houses for invalids, why should not God gather up at last His own invalids? Time passed, and confirmed him in this conviction. The old man grew accustomed to his tower, to the lantern, to the rock, to the sand-bars, to solitude. He grew accustomed also to the sea-mews which hatched in the crevices of the rock, and in the evening held meetings on the roof of the light- house. Skavinski threw to them generally the remnants of his food; and soon they grew tame, and afterward, when he fed them, a real storm of white wings encircled him, and the old man went among the birds like a shepherd among sheep. When the tide ebbed he went to the low sand-banks, on which he collected savory periwinkles and beautiful pearl shells of the nautilus, which receding waves had left on the sand. In the night by the moonlight and the tower he went to catch fish, which frequented the windings of the cliff in myriads. At last he was in love with his rocks and his treeless little island, grown over only with small thick plants exuding sticky resin. The distant views repaid him for the poverty of the island, however. During afternoon hours, when the air became very clear he could see the whole isthmus covered with the richest vegetation. It seemed to Skavinski at such times that he saw one gigantic garden,--bunches of cocoa, and enormous musa, combined as it were in luxurious tufted bouquets, right there behind the houses of Aspinwall. Farther on, between Aspinwall and Panama, was a great forest over which every morning and evening hung a reddish haze of exhalations,--a real tropical forest with its feet in stagnant water, interlaced with lianas and filled with the sound of one sea of gigantic orchids, palms, milk-trees, iron-trees, gum-trees.

Through his field-glass the old man could see not only trees and the broad leaves of bananas, but even legions of monkeys and great marabous and flocks of parrots, rising at times like a rainbow cloud over the forest. Skavinski knew such forests well, for after being wrecked on the Amazon he had wandered whole weeks among similar arches and thickets. He had seen how many dangers and deaths lie concealed under those wonderful and smiling exteriors. During the nights which he had spent in them he heard close at hand the sepulchral voices of howling monkeys and the roaring of the jaguars; he saw gigantic serpents coiled like lianas on trees; he knew those slumbering forest lakes full of torpedo-fish and swarming with crocodiles; he knew under what a yoke man lives in those unexplored wildernesses in which are single leaves that exceed a man's size ten times,--wildernesses swarming with blood-drinking mosquitoes, tree-leeches, and gigantic poisonous spiders. He had experienced that forest life himself, had witnessed it, had passed through it; therefore it gave him the greater enjoyment to look from his height and gaze on those matos, admire their beauty, and be guarded from their treacherousness. His tower preserved him from every evil. He left it only for a few hours on Sunday. He put on then his blue keeper's coat with silver buttons, and hung his crosses on his breast. His milk-white head was raised with a certain pride when he heard at the door, while entering the church, the Creoles say among themselves, "We have an honorable light-house keeper and not a heretic, though he is a Yankee." But he returned straightway after Mass to his island, and returned happy, for he had still no faith in the mainland. On Sunday also he read the Spanish newspaper which he brought in the town, or the New York Herald, which he borrowed from Falconbridge; and he sought in it European news eagerly. The poor old heart on that light-house tower, and in another hemisphere, was beating yet for its birthplace. At times too, when the boat brought his daily supplies and water to the island, he went down from the tower to talk with Johnson, the guard. But after a while he seemed to grow shy. He ceased to go to the town to read the papers and to go down to talk politics with Johnson. Whole weeks passed in this way, so that no one saw him and he saw no one. The only signs that the old man was living were the disappearance of the provisions left on shore, and the light of the lantern kindled every evening with the same regularity with which the sun rose in the morning from the waters of those regions. Evidently, the old man had become indifferent to the world. Homesickness was not the cause, but just this,--that even homesickness had passed into resignation. The whole world began now and ended for Skavinski on his island. He had grown accustomed to the thought that he would not leave the tower till his death, and he simply forgot that there was anything else besides it. Moreover, he had become a mystic; his mild blue eyes began to stare like the eyes of a child, and were as if fixed on something at a distance. In presence of a surrounding uncommonly simple and great, the old man was losing the feeling of personality; he was ceasing to exist as an individual, was becoming merged more and more in that which inclosed him. He did not understand anything beyond his environment; he felt only unconsciously. At last it seems to him that the heavens, the water, his rock, the tower, the golden sand-banks, and the swollen sails, the sea-mews, the ebb and flow of the tide,--all form a mighty unity, one enormous mysterious soul; that he is sinking in that mystery, and feels that soul which lives and lulls itself. He sinks and is rocked, forgets himself; and in that narrowing of his own individual existence, in that half- waking, half-sleeping, he has discovered a rest so great that it nearly resembles half-death.

# CHAPTER III.

But the awakening came.

On a certain day, when the boat brought water and a supply of provisions, Skavinski came down an hour later from the tower, and saw that besides the usual cargo there was an additional package. On the outside of this package were postage stamps of the United States, and the address: "Skavinski, Esq.," written on coarse canvas.

The old man, with aroused curiosity, cut the canvas, and saw books; he took one in his hand, looked at it, and put it back; thereupon his hands began to tremble greatly. He covered his eyes as if he did not believe them; it seemed to him as if he were dreaming. The book was Polish,-- what did that mean? Who could have sent the book? Clearly, it did not occur to him at the first moment that in the beginning of his light- house career he had read in the Herald, borrowed from the consul, of the formation of a Polish society in New York, and had sent at once to that society half his month's salary, for which he had, moreover, no use on the tower. The society had sent him the books with thanks. The books came in the natural way; but at the first moment the old man could not seize those thoughts. Polish books in Aspinwall, on his tower, amid his solitude,--that was for him something uncommon, a certain breath from past times, a kind of miracle. Now it seemed to him, as to those sailors in the night, that something was calling him by name with a voice greatly beloved and nearly forgotten. He sat for a while with closed eyes, and was almost certain that, when he opened them, the dream would be gone.

The package, cut open, lay before him, shone upon clearly by the afternoon sun, and on it was an open book. When the old man stretched his hand toward it again, he heard in the stillness the beating of his own heart. He looked; it was poetry. On the outside stood printed in great letters the title, underneath the name of the author. The name was not strange to Skavinski; he saw that it belonged to the great poet,[1] whose productions he had read in 1830 in Paris. Afterward, when campaigning in Algiers and Spain, he had heard from his countrymen of the grow-

---

1  Mickiewicz (pronounced Mitskyevich), the greatest poet of Poland.

ing fame of the great seer; but he was so accustomed to the musket at that time that he took no book in hand. In 1849 he went to America, and in the adventurous life which he led he hardly ever met a Pole, and never a Polish book. With the greater eagerness, therefore, and with a livelier beating of the heart, did he turn to the title-page. It seemed to him then that on his lonely rock some solemnity is about to take place. Indeed it was a moment of great calm and silence. The clocks of Aspinwall were striking five in the afternoon. Not a cloud darkened the clear sky; only a few sea-mews were sailing through the air. The ocean was as if cradled to sleep. The waves on the shore stammered quietly, spreading softly on the sand. In the distance the white houses of Aspinwall, and the wonderful groups of palm, were smiling. In truth, there was something there solemn, calm, and full of dignity. Suddenly, in the midst of that calm of Nature, was heard the trembling voice of the old man, who read aloud as if to understand himself better:

"Thou art like health, O my birth-land Litva![2]
How much we should prize thee he only can know who has lost thee.
Thy beauty in perfect adornment this day
I see and describe, because I am yearning for thee."

His voice failed Skavinski. The letters began to dance before his eyes; something broke in his breast, and went like a wave from his heart higher and higher, choking his voice and pressing his throat. A moment more he controlled himself, and read further:

"O Holy Lady, who guardest bright Chenstohova,
Who shinest in Ostrobrama and preservest
The castle town Novgrodek with its trusty people,
As Thou didst give me back to health in childhood,
When by my weeping mother placed beneath Thy care
I raised my lifeless eyelids upward,
And straightway walked unto Thy holy threshold,
To thank God for the life restored me,--

---

2   Lithuania.

So by a wonder now restore us to the bosom of our birthplace."

The swollen wave broke through the restraint of his will. The old man sobbed, and threw himself on the ground; his milk-white hair was mingled with the sand of the sea. Forty years had passed since he had seen his country, and God knows how many since he heard his native speech; and now that speech had come to him itself,--it had sailed to him over the ocean, and found him in solitude on another hemisphere,--it so loved, so dear, so beautiful! In the sobbing which shook him there was no pain,-- only a suddenly aroused immense love, in the presence of which other things are as nothing. With that great weeping he had simply implored forgiveness of that beloved one, set aside because he had grown so old, had become so accustomed to his solitary rock, and had so forgotten it that in him even longing had begun to disappear. But now it returned as if by a miracle; therefore the heart leaped in him.

Moments vanished one after another; he lay there continually. The mews flew over the light-house, crying as if alarmed for their old friend. The hour in which he fed them with the remnants of his food had come; therefore, some of them flew down from the light-house to him; then more and more came, and began to pick and to shake their wings over his head. The sound of the wings roused him. He had wept his fill, and had now a certain calm and brightness; but his eyes were as if inspired. He gave unwittingly all his provisions to the birds, which rushed at him with an uproar, and he himself took the book again. The sun had gone already behind the gardens and the forest of Panama, and was going slowly beyond the isthmus to the other ocean; but the Atlantic was full of light yet; in the open air there was still perfect vision; therefore, he read further:

"Now bear my longing soul to those forest slopes, to those green meadows."

At last the dusk obliterates the letters on the white paper,--the dusk short as a twinkle. The old man rested his head on the rock, and closed his eyes. Then "She who defends bright Chenstohova" took his soul, and transported it to "those fields colored by various grain." On the sky were burning yet those long stripes, red and golden, and on those brightnesses he was flying to beloved regions. The pine-woods were sounding in his ears; the streams of his native place were murmuring. He saw everything as it was; everything asked him, "Dost remember?" He remembers! he sees broad fields; between the fields, woods and villages. It is night now. At this hour his lantern usually illuminates the darkness of the sea; but now he is in his native village. His old head has dropped on his breast, and he is dreaming. Pictures are passing before his eyes quickly, and a little disorderly. He does not see the house in which he was born, for war had destroyed it; he does not see his father and mother, for they died when he was a child; but still the village is as if he had left it yesterday,--the line of cottages with lights in the windows, the mound, the mill, the two ponds opposite each other, and thundering all night with a chorus of frogs. Once he had been on guard in that village all night; now that past stood before him at once in a series of views. He is an Ulan again, and he stands there on guard; at a distance is the public-house; he looks with swimming eyes. There is thundering and singing and shouting amid the silence of the night with voices of fiddles and bass-viols "U-ha! U-ha!" Then the Ulans knock out fire with their horseshoes, and it is wearisome for him there on his horse. The hours drag on slowly; at last the lights are quenched; now as far as the eye reaches there is mist, and mist impenetrable; now the fog rises, evidently from the fields, and embraces the whole world with a whitish cloud. You would say, a complete ocean. But that is fields; soon the land-rail will be heard in the darkness, and the bitterns will call from the reeds. The night is calm and cool,--in truth, a Polish night! In the distance the pine-wood is sounding without wind, like the roll of the sea. Soon dawn will whiten the East. In fact, the cocks are beginning to crow behind the hedges. One answers to another from cottage to cottage; the storks are screaming somewhere on high. The Ulan feels well and bright. Some one had spoken of a battle to-morrow. Hei! that will go on, like all the others, with shouting, with fluttering of flaglets. The young blood is playing like a trumpet, though the night cools it. But it is dawning. Already night is growing pale; out of the shadows come forests, the thicket, a row of cottages, the mill, the poplars. The well is squeaking like a metal banner on a tower. What a beloved land, beautiful in the rosy gleams of the morning! Oh, the one land, the one land!

Quiet! the watchful picket hears that some one is approaching. Of course, they are coming to relieve the guard.

Suddenly some voice is heard above Skavinski,--

"Here, old man! Get up! What's the matter?"

The old man opens his eyes, and looks with wonder at the person standing before him. The remnants of the dream-visions struggle in his head with reality. At last the visions pale and vanish. Before him stands Johnson, the harbor guide.

"What's this?" asked Johnson; "are you sick?"

"No."

"You didn't light the lantern. You must leave your place. A vessel from St. Geromo was wrecked on the bar. It is lucky that no one was drowned, or you would go to trial. Get into the boat with me; you'll hear the rest at the Consulate."

The old man grew pale; in fact he had not lighted the lantern that night.

A few days later, Skavinski was seen on the deck of a steamer, which was going from Aspinwall to New York. The poor man had lost his place. There opened before him new roads of wandering; the wind had torn that leaf away again to whirl it over lands and seas, to sport with it till satisfied. The old man had failed greatly during those few days, and was bent over; only his eyes were gleaming. On his new road of life he held at his breast his book, which from time to time he pressed with his hand as if in fear that that too might go from him.

# THE PLAIN SISTER
## BY
## DEMETRIOS BIKELAS

## I.

Mr. Plateas, professor of Greek in the Gymnasium of Syra, was returning from his regular afternoon walk.

He used to take this walk along the Vaporia, but since they had begun to build a carriage road to Chroussa--at the other end of the island--he bent his steps in that direction, instead of pacing four times up and down the only promenade in Syra. He followed the road-building with great interest, and went farther and farther from week to week. His learned colleagues said he would finally get to Chroussa,--when the road was finished; but at this time--that is, in 1850--the Conservative party in the town regarded the expense as useless and too heavy for the resources of the commune, and so the work had been stopped for some months.

The road was completed as far as the stony valley of Mana, and here the professor's daily walk ended. To look at him nobody would have suspected that he had to care for his health; but his growing stoutness gave him no little anxiety, and led him to take this exercise. Perhaps his short stature made him look stouter than he really was; yet it could not be denied that his neck emerged with difficulty from the folds of his neck- cloth, or that his close-shaven, brick-red cheeks stood out rather too conspicuously on each side of his thick moustache. The professor had passed his fortieth year. True, he still preserved his elasticity, and his short legs carried their burden easily; but it was noticed that when he had a companion on his walks, he always contrived to have his interlocutor do the talking going up hill, and took his own turn coming down or on the level ground.

If he had thus far failed to lessen his rotundity, he had at least stopped its growth,--a fact of which he made sure once a month by weighing himself on the scales of the Custom House, where a friend of his held the post of weigher. His physician had also recommended sea- bathing. Most of his friends--both doctors and laymen--protested against this advice; but the professor was immovable when once he had made up his mind or bestowed his confidence; he stood firm against the remonstrance and banter of those who regarded sea-bathing as a tonic, and consequently fattening. He continued his baths for two seasons, and would have kept on for the rest of his life, if a dreadful accident had not given him such a fear of the sea, that he would have risked doubling his circumference rather than expose himself again to the danger from which he had been saved only through the strength and courage of Mr. Liakos, a judge of the civil court. But for him, Mr. Plateas would have been drowned, and this history unwritten.

It happened in this wise.

The professor was not an expert swimmer, but he could keep above water, and was particularly fond of floating. One summer day as he lay on the surface of the tepid sea quite unconcernedly, the sense of comfort led to a slight somnolence. All at once he felt the water heaving under him as if suddenly parted by some heavy body, and then seething against his person. In an instant he thought of a shark, and turned quickly to swim away from the monster; but whether from hurry, fright, or his own weight, he lost his balance and sank heavily. While all this happened quick as a flash, the moments seemed like centuries to him, and his imagination, excited by the sudden rush of blood to the head, worked so swiftly, that, as the professor said afterwards, if he should try to set down everything that came into his mind then, it would make a good-sized book. Scenes of his childhood, incidents of his youth, the faces of his favorite pupils since the beginning of his career as a teacher, the death of his mother, the breakfast he had eaten that morning,--all passed before him in quick succession, and mingled together without becoming confused; while as a musical accompaniment, there kept sounding in his ears the verse of Valaoritis in "The Bell":

"Ding-dong! The bell!"

The night before poor Mr. Plateas had been reading "The Bell" of the poet of Leucadia,--that pathetic picture of the enamored young sailor, who, on returning to his village, throws himself into the sea to reach more speedily the shore, where he hears the tolling knell and sees the funeral procession of his beloved, and as he buffets the waves is devoured by the monster of the deep. The poetical description of this catastrophe had so affected him that he afterwards attributed his misadventure to the influence of the poet's verses. If he had not read "The Bell" that night, he would not have mistaken for a shark the urchin that swam under him, for it was not the first time that mischievous boys had amused themselves by plunging under the professor's broad shoulders; but he had never been frightened before, while to-day this poetic recollection nearly cost him his life.

Fortunately Mr. Liakos was taking his bath near by, and when he saw the professor disappear in that extraordinary fashion, and the circles widening on the surface, he at once understood what had happened. Swimming rapidly to the spot, he dived down, managed to grasp the drowning man, dragged him to the surface, and brought him ashore unconscious. Thanks to these prompt measures, Mr. Plateas came to himself,--with great difficulty, it is true, but he finally did come to himself; and there on the shore of the sea he made a double vow: never again to go into the water, and never to forget that he owed his life to Mr. Liakos.

This vow he kept faithfully. Indeed, so far as his preserver was concerned, it was kept with such exaggeration, that while the judge did not repent saving the professor's life, he often found himself regretting that some one else had not been at hand to earn all this embarrassing gratitude. Everywhere Mr. Plateas boasted of the merits of his preserver; the whole island resounded with his praise; each time they met,--and they met several times a day,--he rushed toward the judge enthusiastically and lost no chance to proclaim that henceforth his only desire was to prove his words by his deeds. "My life belongs to you," he would say; "I have consecrated it to you."

In vain the judge protested, and urged that the matter was not so serious,--that any one else would have done the same in his place. Mr. Plateas would not be convinced, and persisted in declaring his gratitude. While it often rather bored him, the judge was touched by this devotion, and came to accept the professor as a part of his daily life; in this way the two men gradually became fast friends, although they were unlike in almost everything.

So Mr. Plateas was returning from his constitutional. It was one of those beautiful February days, true forerunners of spring, when the sun kisses the first leaves of the early almonds, the blue sea sparkles, and the cloudless sky of Greece smiles. But it was nearly sunset, and the prudent professor hardly dared expose himself to the cool evening air, for at this season winter reasserts itself as soon as the sun goes down. He had almost reached the dockyard, which then marked the outskirts of Syra, and was still walking along the shore, when he saw his well- beloved Liakos in the distance coming from the town. A smile of satisfaction lighted his round face; he threw up both hands, in one of which was a stout cane, and raising his voice so as to be heard by his friend from afar, declaimed this line from the "Iliad":

Who mayest thou be, of mortal men most brave?

The professor had a habit of quoting Homer on all occasions, and was reputed to know the whole "Iliad" and "Odyssey" by heart. He modestly disavowed this tribute to his learning, but without giving up the quotations that seemed to justify it. It is true ill-natured people said his verses were not always quite applicable; but the Hellenists of Syra did not confirm this slander, possibly because they were not competent to judge. Still, everybody used to smile when he raised his voice in the midst of a trivial conversation to roll forth majestically some sonorous hexameter from Homer.

When the two friends were near enough, Mr. Plateas stopped and effusively shook hands with his preserver.

"My dear friend, why didn't you tell me you were going to walk to-day? We could have come out together,--it's time to go in now. Why did you start so late?"

"Yes, I am late; I expected to meet you farther on." And Mr. Liakos added with a show of indifference, "Are there many people out to-day?"

"Very few. You know our Syrans; they're content to saunter up and down their crowded square; it is only people of taste who enjoy themselves--

... on the shore of the resounding sea."

"And who were these men of taste to-day?" asked the judge, with a smile.

"If I had spoken of MEN of taste, I should have had to confine myself to the dual number!" Mr. Plateas began to laugh at his own joke. His friend smiled too, but wishing a more exact answer, continued:

"At least we two have imitators; how many did you meet and who were they?"

"Always the same; Mr. A., Mr. B.--" And the professor began to count off on his fingers the peripatetic philosophers, as he used to call the frequenters of this promenade, that he had met,--all of them old, or at least of ripe age, except one romantic youth who thought himself a poet.

"And no ladies?" asked the judge.

"Oh, yes, Mrs. X. with her flock of children, and the merchant,--what is his name,--Mr. Mitrophanis, with his two daughters."

The judge had learned all he wanted to know without letting his friend perceive the drift of his questions. This was not very difficult, for the professor was by no means a modern Lynceus, and did not see any great distance beyond his nose. No doubt this resulted from the innate simplicity and integrity of his character; having never been able to conceal or feign anything himself, he was easily led to believe whatever he was told. The readiness with which he became the victim of his friends each first of April was notorious. He was always on the watch from the night before; but his precautions were in vain. He was a man of first impressions. Sometimes, but not often, he fathomed the questions afterward, and discovered that he had not acted or spoken as he would have liked. As a rule, however, these after-thoughts came too late to be of any use, and he had to console himself with the reflection that what's done is done.

"What do you say, will you stroll on with me?" asked the judge.

"What, at this hour, my dear friend!"

"Only to the turn of the road."

"You had better come home with me, and I'll treat you to some perfumed wine that I received yesterday from Siphnos. I can recommend it."

"Well, since you are so kind, I shall be very glad to taste your native wine; but first let us sit here awhile and breathe the fresh sea-air." And he pointed to a modest cafe, "On the Sands," which a bold speculator had improvised only a few weeks before, by making a small inclosure of planks and setting up a few tables.

The professor turned toward the cafe, then looked at the setting sun, took out his watch, glanced at the hour, and heaved a gentle sigh.

"You do whatever you please with me," he said, as he followed Mr. Liakos.

# II.

The two friends bent their steps toward the empty cafe, to the great delight of the proprietor, who ran forward zealously to offer his services. The judge contrived to place the seats so that he could see the road that led to Mana. The professor sat down opposite, facing the town, with his back to the country; but he seemed rather nervous about the evening air, for he shivered every now and then, and took care to button up his overcoat to the very neck.

They began by talking about their daily affairs; Mr. Liakos suggested the topics, while the professor held forth to his heart's content, and fairly revelled in Homeric quotation. He noticed, however, that his companion, instead of heeding what he said, kept looking toward the highway, and leaning forward to see still further around the bend in the road. Following his friend's gaze, Mr. Plateas also turned now and then; he even turned squarely around and peered through his glasses to find out what the judge was looking at; but seeing nothing he sat down again erect upon his stool, and went on with the conversation.

At last Mr. Liakos espied what he was looking for. His eyes shone; the expression of his whole face changed, and he made no further pretence of listening to his friend's story about a recent controversy between two learned professors in the University of Athens. Seeing the judge's eyes fixed upon some object behind, Mr. Plateas stopped short, leaned his fat hand on the table to aid the gyration that he was about to make upon his stool, and was preparing for another effort to discover what could thus fascinate Mr. Liakos, when the judge, divining his companion's purpose, suddenly laid his hand on the professor's, and pressing it firmly, said in a low voice, but with a tone of authority:

"Don't turn around!"

Mr. Plateas sat motionless, with mouth open and eyes fastened on those of his friend, who was still staring at the road. The judge's look showed that the object of his interest was coming nearer, but the professor did not dare to stir or utter a word.

"Talk," whispered Mr. Liakos. "Continue the conversation."

"But, my dear friend, what shall I say? You've driven every idea out of my head."

"Recite something."

"What shall I recite?"

"Anything you like,--something out of the 'Iliad.'"

"But I can't think of a single line!"

"Say the Creed, then,--anything you please, only don't sit there dumb."

The poor professor began to stammer out mechanically the first words of the Creed; but either from a sense of impiety or from mere confusion of mind, he passed abruptly to the first book of the "Iliad." His memory played him false. How his pupils would have suffered if they had thus maltreated the immortal bard!

He was still reciting when the judge released his hand and got up to make an elaborate bow. Mr. Plateas looked in the same direction, and saw the back of an elderly gentleman between two attractive young girls. He had no difficulty in recognizing the trio, even from the rear.

Mr. Liakos sat down again, blushing furiously while the professor in utter stupefaction made the sign of the cross.

"Kyrie Eleison!" said he. "Then all this ado was for Mr. Mitrophanis and his daughters?"

"I beg your pardon," replied the judge, in a voice that betrayed his agitation. "I did not want them to think that we were talking about them."

"Bless my soul! You don't mean to say you're in love?"

"Ah, yes. I love her with all my heart!" Mr. Liakos turned once more, and his eyes followed one of the two girls.

The professor had listened with some uneasiness. While touched by the judge's emotion, he was at the same time perhaps a little jealous of its cause; he was surprised that his friend had never spoken of this love, and vexed with himself that he had not divined it. But all these ideas were so hazy that he could hardly have expressed them.

After a few moments' silence, and while the judge's passionate avowal still lingered in his ears, he asked naively, and without stopping to think:

"Which one?"

Mr. Liakos looked at the professor in astonishment, and although he did not speak, the expression of his face said plainly, "Can you ask?"

Mr. Plateas clapped his hand to his forehead.

"Where were my wits!" he cried. "Excuse me, my dear friend; but seeing only their backs, as I did a moment ago, I couldn't tell one from the other; and I had forgotten that the elder sister's face would scarcely inspire love. But the younger--SHE is charming!"

The judge listened without reply.

"Do you know," the professor went on, at last unburdening his mind, "I don't understand how you could be in love, and not tell me about it; how you could hide your feelings from your friend! If it had been I, you wouldn't have been spared a single sigh!" And his chest gave forth an "Ah" which he tried to render amorous. This sigh, or perhaps the mere idea of the professor in love, brought a smile to the judge's clouded face.

"Why haven't you ever spoken to me about it?" continued Mr. Plateas.

"Because I did not wish to bore you," replied Mr. Liakos. Then, touched by his friend's reproachful look, he made haste to add, "But now I will tell you everything, since you desire it."

Still he was silent, as if he hardly knew how to begin. The professor shivered again, and seeing that the sun had gone down behind the mountains, said:

"Hadn't we better talk about this on the way home, or at my house? It's time to go in."

The two men rose, and started toward the city.

What desponding lover has not yearned to pour out his heart to some friend? Even reverence for the purity of his feeling will not restrain him. He tries to guard the mystery of his love as in a holy sanctuary; he would not expose it to unrevering eyes; he hesitates, he delays,-- but sooner or later his heart will overflow, and he must have a confidant.

The judge had already chosen his confidant, and so was in no hurry to take advantage of the opportunity that now offered; he was still silent, and began to regret his thoughtless promise to tell his friend everything. While he had an esteem and even a warm affection for Mr. Plateas, he could not regard the professor as a fitting recipient for a love-confidence, or quite able to appreciate the delicacy of his feeling; and, besides, it seemed to him almost treason to reveal again the secret he had already confided to another.

Mr. Plateas noticed his friend's hesitancy, but ascribed it to agitation. After a pause he saw that the confession was not coming of itself, and tried to draw it out by asking questions. Although frank, the answers he received were brief; still, he was able to gather that the judge had been in love ever since coming to Syra,--three years before,--and had then vowed either to marry Mr. Mitrophanis's younger daughter, or never to marry at all. It was only within the last few months, however, that Mr. Liakos had met the young girl for the first time, at a friend's house, and had discovered that his love was returned.

"Where did this happen?"

"At my cousin's."

"Does she know the two girls?"

"Oh, yes; she was a friend of their mother's."

"Ah! Now I understand," cried the professor. "Your cousin received your sighs. She has been your confidante! That's why you never said anything to me."

The judge smiled, but his poor friend felt a little jealous of this cousin.

"Why didn't you propose for her hand just as soon as you knew she liked you?" the professor continued.

"I did, a week ago; I requested my cousin to call on Mr. Mitrophanis, but--"

"But what? Where could he find a better son-in-law? He didn't refuse you, surely?"

"No, he did not refuse, but he made a condition that can be fulfilled-- Heaven knows when! In the meanwhile he does not wish us to meet. I had not seen her for ten days, even at a distance, and you can understand with what emotion just now I--"

"What is this condition?" asked the professor.

"To wait until the elder sister is married. He won't allow the younger to marry, or even to be betrothed, before the elder."

"Ah, my friend, that's a pity! I fear you'll have to wait a long, long time. It won't be so easy to marry off the sister. Still, all things are possible,--you mustn't despair."

The judge was silent, evidently a prey to melancholy. After a little he said:

"And yet that sister is a perfect treasure, in spite of her lack of beauty. There isn't a sweeter soul on earth; she has entreated her father to change his decision; she assures him that she has no wish to marry, and that her only desire is to remain with him to care for his old age, and to help rear her sister's children. But the old man is inflexible; when once he takes a stand, that's the end of it!"

The judge's tongue was untied, and he was as eloquent in praise of the elder sister as he had been reserved in telling of his love. Perhaps this eased his mind, for to speak of her seemed almost like speaking of his sweetheart; to commend the one was to exalt the other.

"She is an angel of goodness," he continued, "and loves her sister with all a mother's tenderness; indeed, she has filled a mother's place ever since the two girls were left orphans. She has the whole care of the house, and manages it admirably; my cousin never tires of telling me that she has nowhere seen such good order, or a house so well kept. But you must not imagine that she neglects other things for the sake of her housekeeping. Few of our women are so well read or so widely informed. In that respect, at least, Mr. Mitrophanis is worthy of all praise; his daughters have been carefully educated. It is hardly his fault if the two are not equally fair to look upon; in beauty of character they are equal. The elder also is a treasure, and happy the man that wins her."

At first the professor listened in some astonishment to his friend's sudden enthusiasm; then, little by little, his surprise changed to uneasiness. He began to suspect that--But he was not the man to conceal anything that came into his mind, and stopping abruptly in the middle of the road, he interrupted the judge's eulogy.

"But why do you tell me all this?" he asked. "Why do you sing her praises to me? What do you mean--are you trying to inveigle me into marrying her?"

Mr. Liakos was astounded. The idea had never occurred to him; he had never thought of the professor as a marrying man. And yet, why not? In what was he lacking? Wasn't his friend the very man to become the brother-in-law he so ardently desired? All this passed vaguely through his mind while he stood staring at Mr. Plateas, unable to find an answer to this unexpected question. The professor continued with energy:

"Listen, Liakos. I owe you my life; it belongs to you. But if you ask me to get married as a proof of my gratitude, I'd far rather go this moment back to the sea, where you saved me from death, and drown myself before your very eyes!"

The sudden heat of the professor's speech showed that he was hurt, but whether at what the judge had just been saying about the elder sister, or at the secrecy he had shown in the matter and his studied reserve in speaking of the younger sister, was doubtful. Probably the good man himself did not know; what he did know was that he felt hurt. This was clear enough from what he said and the way he said it.

Mr. Liakos was offended.

"Mr. Plateas," he replied dryly, "I have often told you--and I repeat it now for the last time, I hope--I have not, and I do not wish to have, any claim upon your gratitude. As for your marrying, I assure you that I never dreamed of presenting you as a suitor, or of seeking a wife for you. I had not the least thought of it when I spoke to you of my affairs, and I now regret having troubled you with them."

The two friends walked on in silence side by side, but were impatient to part as soon as they could decorously. When they had nearly reached the place where their homeward paths would separate, the professor repeated his invitation.

"Won't you come and taste my muscat?"

"No, thank you; it is late, and I have an engagement."

"With your cousin, perhaps?"

"Perhaps!" and the judge tried to smile.

"I hope you're not vexed with me," said his friend, in a conciliatory tone.

"Why should I be?"

"Perhaps what I said was uncalled for,--particularly as you never meant to interfere with my liberty." The good man began to laugh, and then added: "But it's much better to have such things cleared up."

"Certainly, quite so."

The judge shook the fat hand that was cordially offered him, and hurried on, while his companion went slowly home.

# III.

The professor's house was on the hillside in the quarter where the Orphan Asylum now stands. At that time there were very few dwellings in the neighborhood, which was rather far from the centre of the town, and the outlook was wide and varied. It was not the view, however, that had attracted the professor, but the cheapness of the land. He had built the house himself, and its walls were the fruit of many years of toil. Small and modest as it was, it was his own; he was in debt to no man, and had no rent to pay. This sweet feeling of independence quite made up for the tiring climb that the corpulent little owner had to take twice a day up the steep "River," as the street was called. The road bore this name (as everybody knows who has visited Syra), because it had been the bed of a stream that used to carry the winter rains from the mountain to the sea. In fact, the water runs down the street to this day, and in the wet season it becomes a raging torrent. Although the rocks and stones that once lined its sides have given place to houses, with their doors raised high above the flood, the origin of the street and the reason for its name are obvious enough even now.

Fortunately, rains are rare in Syra, but when they do fall, the "River" is often impassable; at such times the professor could reach his house only by zigzags through the side streets, and there were days when all communication was cut off, and he had to stay shut up at home.

The greatest pleasure that the house had brought him was that it had enabled him to give his old mother the happiness of passing her last days in comfort under her own roof, after the long privations and trials through which she had reared her son and had seen him overcome the difficulties of his professorial career. She had died peacefully in this house, and although a year had passed, her room remained as she had left it. The professor really needed it for his library, which grew from day to day, but he preferred to leave the room unused, as sacred to his mother's memory.

The only heritage that she left him was her old servant, the taciturn Florou, whose senile caprices he endured patiently, bearing with her uncertain service and poor cooking. Florou's rule, however, rose no higher than the ground-floor. Her master found peace and quiet in his own room upstairs. Here he worked; at his table before the window he prepared his lessons, and read his favorite authors. Here, with pen in hand and his books spread out before him, he liked to look dreamily over the roofs of the other houses at the sea and the hazy outline of the neighboring islands, or to lean back with closed eyelids and look--at nothing, for he was asleep.

The professor was very fond of his house. Since he had owned it, he went out but little except to attend to his classes or take his regular walk, and it was always with a new pleasure that he looked upon his walls and opened his door again.

This evening he came home with even greater contentment than usual, as to a haven of refuge from the fancied dangers that lurked in his friend's eulogy of the plain sister.

"That would be the finishing stroke!" he said aloud, as he carefully folded his coat, put on an old dressing-gown, and tied a silk handkerchief around his head in the shape of a cap, as was his custom every evening.

"That would be the finishing stroke indeed! To bring a wife here to turn everything upside down; to take me out when I want to stay in, or keep me in when I want to go out; to talk to me when I want quiet; to open the window when I am chilly, because she is too warm; or to close it when I am warm, because she is too cold!" and with that he shut the window.

"Marriage may be all very well for the young; but when a man has reached years of discretion, such folly is not to be thought of. I have escaped the fetters so far, and I am not going to throw away my liberty at this late day!

Craftily they contrived against my freedom,"

He remembered the woman who had been chosen for him in his youth, as he had seen her the year before while on a visit to his native island,-- with her gray hair and premature wrinkles,--surrounded by a troop of children, playing, quarrelling, and crying.

"Thank Heaven," he said aloud, "I haven't that load to carry! I wish the man joy that fills my place!"

Florou interrupted him by opening the door. She looked about the room in astonishment, but seeing that her master was only talking to himself, she shook her head and said curtly:

"Supper!"

"Very well, I'm coming;" and he went down to the parlor, which was next to the kitchen and served as dining-room also. The professor sat down with a good appetite, and when his hunger was appeased, he began to think over the incidents of his walk. At first his mind dwelt upon the advantages of bachelorhood; then he thought of Mr. Liakos, and felt a sincere pity for his friend.

"Poor fellow!" he said to himself. "He has been hit by Cupid's arrow, and is no longer his own master. He thinks he's on the right road to happiness; I hope he may find it, and never discover his mistake! Well, we never get just what we want in this world, and a man's happiness depends after all on his own way of feeling and thinking."

Mr. Plateas fancied this was philosophy, but, in fact, it was only a blind attempt to get rid of disagreeable thoughts. He could not forget the judge's evident dejection and vain effort to hide it. What if Mr. Liakos did want him to marry the plain sister! Perhaps his friend had felt a delicacy about speaking to him on the subject, and had denied ever having thought of such a thing only when stung by his ungrateful words.

Who had a better right to claim such a sacrifice? Did he not owe his very life to the judge? And how had he repaid this debt? He had tried to escape it! He had ignored his friend's delicacy, and basely threatened to drown himself rather than lift a hand to secure his preserver's happiness. The more he thought of it, the blacker seemed his ingratitude. He had actually insulted the man who had saved his life! The blood rushed to his cheeks; his remorse grew keener and keener, and his philosophy was of little comfort. Having eaten his last bunch of raisins, be pushed away his plate angrily, threw his napkin on the table, and went up to his room in a very discontented frame of mind.

"I've behaved abominably," he said to himself. "Why should I have offended him? There was no need of saying what I did. Reflection always comes too late with me!"

And striking his head with his hand, he paced up and down his room in the growing darkness until Florou came in and put his lamp on the table.

She came and went without a word.

The professor stopped a moment, and his eyes rested on the light. The light reminded him of his duty and invited him to work; he must prepare his lesson for the morrow. For the first time in his life he found that he could not fix his mind upon his books. He hesitated, and then began to walk up and down again, thinking of Mr. Liakos, of his pupils, of the merchant's two daughters, and of the gymnasiarch,[3] all at the same time. Finally, in this jumble of ideas, professional instinct got the upper hand. He sat down at the table, put the three heavy volumes of Gazis's Dictionary, the Syntax of Asopios, and his other handbooks of study in their usual order, then set out his ink and paper, and found in his "Iliad" the page marked for the next day. He began his work by noting the etymology of each word, the syntax of every phrase, and the peculiarities of each hexameter. His class had reached the sixth book of the "Iliad."

Soon, however, he forgot syntax, etymology, and metre; he forgot his pupils and the dry analysis he was making for their benefit, and he read through the passage before him without stopping. It was the parting of Hector and Andromache. He discovered new beauty and meaning in the story; the exquisite picture of conjugal and paternal love, the happiness of mutual affection, the grief of parting, had never made such an impression upon him before. Never before had he read or recited the "Iliad" in this way, for as he read, Mr. Liakos gradually took Hector's place. He kept thinking of his friend; it was his friend who felt the bitterness of separation, and that too without ever having tasted, like Hector, the joys of conjugal happiness!

Mr. Plateas shut his book and started up again. A thousand conflicting thoughts filled his mind as he paced from his table to his bed, and from his bed back to his table.

"Pshaw!" he cried. "Why shouldn't I believe that Liakos never had any thought of marrying me off? I was a fool to imagine such a thing! Do I look like a marrying man?"

He stopped before his glass, which was lighted by the lamp only at one side, and saw one half of his face reflected with the silk handkerchief wound around his head, while the other half was in shadow, and the two ends of the knot stuck up over his forehead.

"Truly," he laughed, "between us we should have a beautiful Astyanax!"

He sat down again, calmer; but once more there began to throng before his eyes scenes and images that had nothing to do with the next day's lesson. He saw that he

---

3   Superintendent of a gymnasium or secondary school.

could not work in earnest, and decided to go to bed, thinking that rest would quiet his nerves, and that he could get up early in the morning and prepare his task with a fresher mind. So he went to bed and put out his lamp. But sleep would not come; he tossed about restlessly, and in the silence and darkness the very tension of his nerves made him more and more remorseful.

The long hours of the night passed slowly. At last, toward morning, he fell asleep; but his waking thoughts were distorted into a frightful nightmare, and he started up in terror. He had dreamt that his bed was the sea, while his pillow was a shark, and his head was in the jaws of the monster. Then the shark began to wear the face and shape of the merchant's elder daughter, and a voice--the voice of Liakos--sounded in his ear, repeating over and over:

"Ding, Dong! Ungrateful wretch! Ding, Dong! Ungrateful wretch!"

He sat up in bed, and as he wiped his dripping forehead with the silk handkerchief, which had come untied in the agony of his dream, he made an heroic resolution.

"I will marry her!" he cried. "I owe so much to my preserver. I must do my duty and ease my conscience."

He covered himself up again, with a lighter heart; his mind was now tranquil, and free from all suspicion, hesitation, or remorse.

The morning sunlight flooded his room and woke him a full hour later than usual. It was the first time this had ever happened to the punctual professor, and Florou was positively dazed. With heavy head and aching eyes, he dressed hastily, swallowed his cup of black coffee, and sat down to the unfinished task of the night before. But his thoughts still wandered.

Nevertheless, he was at the gymnasium in time, and began the daily lesson. But what a lesson! At first the scholars wondered what had become of their teacher's wonted severity; they soon perceived that this remarkable forbearance was not due to any merit on their part, but to complete heedlessness on his. Wonder of wonders! Mr. Plateas was inattentive! Emboldened by this discovery, they took malicious delight in heaping blunder upon blunder, and played dire havoc with that sixth book of the "Iliad," never sparing etymology, syntax, nor prosody. The good man sat through it all undisturbed until the regular closing hour had struck. His pupils went out, commenting not on Homer, but on the unheard-of lenity of their master, while as he walked away he resumed the burden of his thoughts,--how to set about putting his resolve into execution.

The affair was not so simple as it had seemed to him in the night. His decision to marry the elder daughter of Mr. Mitrophanis was not enough; there were certain steps to take, but what were they? Should he apply to his friend? After what had passed between them the day before, he hardly liked to go to the judge and say-- what? "I am ready for the sacrifice!" Certainly he couldn't do that. Should he ask the aid of Mr. Liakos's cousin? There were objections to this course, too; to be sure, he knew the lady, and her husband as well; he was in the habit of bowing to them on the street, but he had never had any conversation with the cousin, and felt that he had neither the right nor the courage to ask her to serve as intermediary.

He thought it all over without reaching any conclusion, and was crossing the square on his way home,--for it was nearly time for his noon-day dinner,--when suddenly he saw Mr. Mitrophanis coming toward him. This meeting put an end to all his doubts, and with a flash of inspiration he decided to speak directly to the young lady's father. What could be simpler? Having no time to weigh the matter carefully, he was only too glad to find this happy way out of his perplexity. He bowed, and stopped before the old gentleman.

"Mr. Mitrophanis, I am delighted to meet you, for I have a few words to say."

"Mr. Plateas, I believe?" said the other, politely returning the bow.

"The same."

"And what can I do for you, Mr. Plateas?"

The professor began to feel a little embarrassed; but it was too late to turn back, so he took courage and went on:

"To come to the point at once, Mr. Mitrophanis, I desire to become your son-in-law!"

This abrupt proposal was a surprise to the old gentleman, and hardly an agreeable one. The offer itself was not so astonishing, for the beauty of his younger daughter had often obliged the father to refuse proposals of this kind; but he had never been addressed quite so brusquely before. Moreover, of all the suitors who had thus far presented themselves, Mr. Plateas seemed the least eligible in point of age and other respects. But it was not this so much that the old gentleman had in mind, as he said to himself, "What, he too!"

"I am greatly honored by your proposal," he said to Mr. Plateas; "but my little girl is too young, and I have not thought of marriage for her yet."

"What little girl? My suit is not for the younger sister; I ask you for the hand of Miss--" He meant to call her by her name, but found he did not know it. "I ask you for the hand of--your elder daughter."

Mr. Mitrophanis could not conceal his astonishment at these words; such a thing had never happened before. He said nothing, but looked sharply at Mr. Plateas, who felt his patience giving way.

"I must admit, Mr. Plateas," said the old gentleman at last, "that your proposition is wholly unexpected, and comes in rather an unusual form. Don't you think that our traditional custom in such cases is very sensible, and that these questions are managed better by intermediaries?"

The professor was not prepared for this. He had even imagined that the young lady's father would fall on his neck in the open street, with delight at having at last found the wished-for son-in-law.

"I--I thought," he stammered, "that you knew me well enough, and that the simplest way was to speak to you myself."

"Certainly, without doubt. But if you would send one of your friends to speak to me, and--give me time for reflection, you would oblige me greatly."

"With pleasure! I'll send Mr. Liakos."

At this name the old man frowned.

"Ah!" said he, "Mr. Liakos is in your confidence."

Poor Mr. Plateas saw that he had made a mistake in bringing up his friend's name in the affair. He was about to say something,--he didn't know exactly what,--when Mr. Mitrophanis forestalled him, and ended his embarrassment.

"It is well. I will await Mr. Liakos." Then the old gentleman bowed and walked on.

Never in his life had the professor been in such a state of mental distress as that to which he had been a prey ever since the evening before. His sufferings at the time he came so near drowning were not to be compared with his present anguish. Then the danger had come suddenly, and he had realized it to the full only when it was over. Now, the uncertainty of the future added to his misery. At the very moment when he thought he had reached port, he found himself completely at sea again. He stood there in the middle of the square, his arms hanging helplessly, and stared at the back of the retreating merchant.

"Well, I must see Liakos." he said to himself. "But where shall I find him at this time of day?"

Just then the clock on the Church of the Transfiguration struck twelve. Mr. Plateas remembered, first that his dinner was waiting for him at home, and next that his friend was in the habit of dining at a certain restaurant behind the square; and wending his way there, he met the judge at the door.

"Oh, my dear friend!" he exclaimed. "My dear friend!"

"What's the matter? What has happened to you?" asked Mr. Liakos, anxiously.

"What has happened to me? Something I never dreamed of! I've just asked Mr. Mitrophanis for the hand of his elder daughter, and instead of---"

"You asked him for his daughter's hand?"

"Yes. Is there anything so very astonishing in that?"

"Why, didn't you tell me yesterday that---"

"Well, what if I did? During the night I thought it over, and became convinced that I ought to get married, and that I never shall find a better wife."

"Listen, Plateas," said Mr. Liakos, obviously much moved. "I understand your sudden conversion, because I understand you; but I can't let you make such a sacrifice."

"What sacrifice? Who said anything about sacrifice? I have made up my mind to get married, because I want to get married; and I WILL get married, and if her father refuses his consent I'll run away with her!" And he gave a lively account of his meeting with Mr. Mitrophanis.

The judge smiled as he listened, for he, too, had been thinking of this match ever since the night before, and the more he thought of it the more eminently fit and proper it seemed. After rigid self-examination, he persuaded himself that he was quite disinterested in the matter, and that his sweetheart's sister and his friend could never be happy apart. As for the father's consent, he had little fear on that score. He rather dreaded, it is true, the mission that was thrust upon him, especially when he thought of the manner in which the old man had received his name; but he felt that he could not refuse this service to his friend, and finally promised to see Mr. Mitrophanis that very day, and to come in the evening to report the happy result of his interview.

# IV.

When the professor had gone, the judge began to think with misgiving of the difficulties that beset his mission. He had so much at stake in its success that his mediation might not be accepted as impartial, or his praise of the suitor as quite unbiased. His friend's cause ought to have been entrusted to some one less deeply interested in the event. If the professor had not been in such haste to name him as an intermediary, they could have consulted his cousin, and even placed the matter in her hands; his own appearance on the scene would only give Mr. Mitrophanis fresh offence.

But why not ask her advice in confidence? She was a woman of sense and experience, and could probably find some way out of their quandary. Mr. Liakos was on the point of going to his cousin, but he reflected that it would be a grave indiscretion to impart the secret to a third person without his friend's consent, and he felt too that it would be very weak in him not to perform loyally the duty that he had undertaken. Forward, then! Courage!

So Mr. Liakos started for the office of his sweetheart's father, although not without inward trepidation.

It so happened that Mr. Mitrophanis was just receiving a consignment of coffee from the Custom House; carts were coming up one after another, porters were carrying the sacks into the warehouse, and the judge had difficulty in making his way to the door.

It was a huge square building, with a room on the street partitioned off at one corner. This room was the office, and had a grated window; but the light from it and from the street door was too dim for Mr. Liakos to see what was going on inside the warehouse. As he stood there on the threshold, he saw that his arrival was ill-timed; for there was a dispute in progress. Although he did not understand, or even try to understand what it was all about, he heard hot words bandied back and forth, and above them he could distinguish the merchant's voice, loud and masterful.

The judge stopped in surprise. He had heard of the old gentleman's temper, but had not imagined that anger could raise to such a pitch a voice usually so calm and dignified. He was alarmed and was trying to slip away unseen, when Mr. Mitrophanis interrupted the discussion and called out to him from the depths of the warehouse:

"What do you wish, Mr. Liakos?"

"I came to say a few words; but I see you're engaged, and will come again some other time."

"Pass into my office, and I will be with you in a moment."

The judge stumbled over some coffee bags, and, making his way into the office, sat down by the merchant's table in the only chair that was vacant. The air was heavy with the odor of colonial merchandise. The dispute began anew inside the warehouse, and the words, "weight," "bags," "Custom House," were repeated over and over again. Mr. Liakos sat listening to the noise, and tried to picture to himself the quiet old gentleman who had been out walking with his two daughters the night before. At last the commotion quieted down, and Mr. Mitrophanis came in with a frown on his face.

"I have happened on an unlucky time for my call," thought the judge.

"I suppose you come from Mr. Plateas," began the old man, with a touch of irony in his tone.

"Yes; the fact is he has communicated to me the conversation he had with you this morning."

"I must say, Mr. Liakos, that your anxiety to find a husband for my elder daughter seems to me rather marked."

"I assure you, sir, that my friend's proposal was wholly voluntary, and was in no wise prompted by me."

The old gentleman smiled incredulously.

"My only regret is," continued the judge, "that I allowed Mr. Plateas to discover my secret yesterday. I protest I never had the least thought of urging him to this step; he has taken it of his own accord, and you do me wrong in supposing that I have acted from self-interest."

"I believe it, since you say so, and will not stop to inquire how it happens that he should ask me for the hand of my daughter, whom he does not know, the very day after receiving your confidence."

"But however that may be," he went on, without letting Mr. Liakos speak, "I cannot give you an immediate reply; I must have time to consider the question. Pray do not trouble yourself to call; I will make my decision known to you." The last words were spoken dryly.

The judge went away much disconcerted. It was not a refusal that he had received, nor yet was it a consent; his most serious disquiet was caused by the old man's tone and manner. Although they might have arisen partly from the dispute in the warehouse, it was only too clear that his deep interest in the success of his mission had been as detrimental in awakening the merchant's suspicions as in checking his own eloquence.

How many things he could have said to Mr. Mitrophanis if he had only dared! He felt that his mediation had simply made matters worse, and might prove fatal. A more skilful diplomatist than he would be needed to conduct the affair to a happy ending; why had he not acted on his first impulse and consulted his cousin? Why not go to her even now? Surely his friend could not be offended, especially if the result was successful; the poor judge was in trouble, and longed for encouragement and support; but while he reasoned with himself, his feet were carrying him to his cousin's house, and by the time he reached her door, all his doubt had vanished.

Mr. Liakos found his kinswoman at work converting a jacket of her elder son, which had become too small for its owner, into a garment still too ample for the younger brother. The boys were at school, while their three sisters--who came between them in age--were studying their lessons under their mother's eye, and at the same time learning domestic economy from her example.

Being a woman of tact, she saw at once from the judge's manner that he wished to speak with her alone, and sent the girls out to play.

"Well, what is it?" she asked as soon as they had left the room. "What's the news?"

"Why should you think there is any news?"

"Ah, indeed! As if I didn't know you! I could see at a glance that you had something on your mind."

In truth, her feminine insight was seldom at fault in reading Mr. Liakos, for she had seen him grow up from a child, and knew him thoroughly. On his side, the judge flattered himself that he knew her quite as well, but then he ought to have foreseen that her help would not be easily enlisted in an affair that she had not been allowed to manage from the beginning. She enjoyed busying herself with marriages in general and with those of her friends in particular; but she felt that she was peculiarly qualified to assume the chief part in planning and carrying out arrangements of this kind, and unless her claims were recognized, she rarely gave her approval, and even did not hesitate to oppose occasionally. But for his discomfiture at the result of his visit to the old merchant, Mr. Liakos would doubtless have devised some way of conciliating his cousin; it had not occurred to him to take that precaution, and he soon perceived the blunder he had made.

When he announced abruptly that he had found a husband for his sweetheart's sister, his cousin, instead of showing pleasure, or at least some curiosity, quietly continued her sewing with affected indifference, saying merely, "Ah!" This "Ah" was half-way between a question and an exclamation; the judge could not tell whether it expressed irony or simple astonishment; but it was enough to chill him.

"Everything is against me!" he thought.

"And who is your candidate?" she asked after a pause, but without stopping her work.

"Mr. Plateas."

His cousin dropped her needle, and looked at Mr. Liakos with eyes full of mocking surprise.

"Mr. Plateas!" she cried, and began to laugh heartily. The judge had never seen her so merry.

"I don't see what you find to laugh at," he said, with dignity.

"You must forgive me," she replied, trying to stifle her merriment. "Pray forgive me if I have hurt you through your friend, but I can't imagine Mr. Plateas in love." And she began to laugh again; then seeing the judge's expression, she asked, "What put this marriage into your head?"

"No," he began, without answering her question, "please to tell me what you find so reprehensible in him."

"Reprehensible!" she repeated, imitating her cousin's tone. "I don't find him reprehensible, simply ridiculous."

"I admit that his person is not awe-inspiring."

"Awe-inspiring! What long words you use! You'll be giving me one of your friend's quotations from Homer next."

"Listen," he said, changing his manner. "At first I looked at it just as you do; but the more I thought it over, the more clearly I saw that I was wrong. Mr. Plateas has all the qualities that go to make a good husband. He will be ridiculous as a lover, I must admit. He will look absurd on his wedding day, with the wreath of flowers on his head[4]---"

At this his cousin broke into a fresh peal of laughter, in which the judge was forced to join in spite of himself. Their sudden gayety having subsided, the conversation became more serious. Mr. Liakos related all the details of the affair, and as his story went on he was delighted to see his cousin's prejudices gradually disappear, although she still made objections when they came to dissect the suitor's character.

"He is a hypochondriac!" she said.

"He takes care of his health," replied the judge, "simply because he has nothing else to occupy him. When once he is married, he'll care for his wife, just as he cared for his mother while she lived and his hypochondria, as you call it, will vanish fast enough."

"He's pedantic."

"That is hardly a grave fault in a professor."

Now that the question had narrowed down to his friend's moral qualities, Mr. Liakos began to feel certain of victory so far as his cousin was concerned. His only remaining doubt was as to the young lady's consent.

"Her consent!" cried his cousin. "She'll accept Mr. Plateas gladly. Since she can't persuade her father to let her remain single, she will take the first husband that offers, rather than stand in the way of her sister's happiness. She has the soul of an angel," the cousin went on, with enthusiasm. "She doesn't know her own worth; she sees that she is not pretty, and in her humility she even exaggerates her plainness; but her sweet unselfishness is no reason why she should be sacrificed."

"Do you think, then, that it would be a sacrifice to marry Mr. Plateas?"

"How can we tell?"

His cousin's reserve was more propitious than her merriment of a few minutes ago, and Mr. Liakos felt encouraged.

"If she were your sister, or even your daughter, would you not give her to

---

4  The Greek bride and bridegroom both wear a wreath of flowers.

him?"

This question struck deeper than he knew, for one of her daughters was not well-favored, and the girl's future was beginning to give the maternal heart much uneasiness. The mother laughed no longer; her eyes filled, and she made no reply. Without searching into the cause of his cousin's emotion, the judge was only too glad to take her silence for consent.

"Very well," he went on. "Now you must help me to arrange this marriage."

In order to humor her innocent vanity, he pictured the obstacles that she would find in the character of Mr. Mitrophanis, and urged his own inability to overcome them; he frankly declared that his mediation had compromised his friend's suit, and that the affair was far more difficult than if it had been in her hands from the beginning; he insisted that she alone could retrieve the mistakes committed, and bring about a happy ending.

His cousin's objections gradually grew weaker and at last, after three hours of argument, the judge succeeded so well that she left her work (to the temporary disadvantage of her younger son), and put on her bonnet. The two went out together, she to call on Mr. Mitrophanis, and he to find the professor.

# V.

Poor Mr. Plateas was waiting for his friend impatiently.

On reaching home he had found his dinner growing cold, and Florou worrying over her master's unusual tardiness; it was full twenty minutes after noon! Although the professor was hungry and ate with relish, his mind was ill at ease. He yearned to talk to some one, but there was no one to talk to. He would have been glad to tell his story even to Florou, but she cared neither to talk nor to listen; conversation was not her strong point.

Besides, her master rather shrank from telling her that be had made up his mind to get married, and that her reign was over. Since his mother's death, Florou had had absolute control over the household; why make her unhappy before it was necessary? On the other hand, he could contain himself no longer; if he had not spoken, there is no telling what would have happened.

Not daring to face the question boldly, he beat about the bush, and tried to pass adroitly from the subject of dinner to that of marriage.

"Florou," he said, "your meat is overdone."

The old woman made no reply, but looked up at the sun as if to suggest that the fault lay not with her, but with her master's tardiness.

He paid no attention to her mute reproach.

"In fact," he went on, "the dinner isn't fit to eat to-day."

"You've eaten it, though."

Florou was in the habit of resorting to this argument as unanswerable. Usually her master laughed and said that he had eaten his dinner because he was hungry, and not because it was good. To-day, however, her phrase irritated him, less on account of the words themselves, than from an inward consciousness that this day of all others he had no right to complain of her culinary art.

In his vexation he forgot how he had planned to lead up to the subject of his marriage, and had to finish his dinner in silence; but while Florou was carrying the dishes away, he thought of a new pretext for coming back to the absorbing topic. He noticed for the first time a hole in the tablecloth that had been there a long time.

"See there!" said he, putting his finger through it. "My house needs a mistress,--there's no other remedy for such a state of things. I must have a wife!"

Florou shrugged her shoulders as though she thought her master had lost his wits.

"Do you understand me? I must get married."

The old woman smiled.

"What are you laughing at? I have quite made up my mind to marry."

Florou stared.

"I'm going to get married, I tell you!"

"And who'll have you?"

"Who will have me!" he cried, fairly choking with rage.

Almost beside himself at the old woman's effrontery, he wanted to crush her with angry eloquence; but her stolidity baffled him, and he went up to his room without a word. When he was alone, his anger soon cooled; but he found himself repeating those cruel words, and as he said them over, he began to fear that Florou was not so far wrong.

He recalled his friend's first disavowal of any thought of him as a suitor, and the father's strange hesitation. And then, why didn't Liakos come; what was keeping him so long? If his mission was successful, he would have brought the news at once. The question was very simple, the answer "yes" or "no"; it surely must be "no," and the judge was keeping back the evil tidings.

How silly he had been to expose himself to a rebuff on the impulse of the moment--what perfect folly! What business had he to get into such a scrape? But no, he had only done his duty; he had proved to his preserver the sincerity of his friendship and the depth of his gratitude. But why didn't Liakos come? Why didn't he hurry back and end this suspense?

The unhappy man looked at his watch again and again, and was astonished each time at the slowness of the hands; they seemed hardly to move at all. He sat down, then jumped up again and looked out of the window,--no Liakos! He tried to read, but could not keep his thoughts from straying, and shut the book petulantly. He was in a perfect fever.

Meanwhile the time came for his daily constitutional, and Mr. Plateas was on thorns. He could not stay indoors waiting for his friend any longer; but in order to be near at hand, he resolved to take his old walk and go no farther than the Vaporia. So he called Florou and told her that he would not be gone long, but that if Mr. Liakos should come, she must send him to the Vaporia. He explained with great care the route he would take in going and in coming back, so that Florou might tell his friend exactly. All this was quite unnecessary, for the road to the Vaporia was so direct that the two friends could hardly help meeting unless they went out of their way to avoid each other; but he insisted upon his topographical directions, and repeated them so often that Florou at last lost her patience, and exclaimed:

"Very well, very well!"

It was most unusual for the old woman to say the same word twice.

Not a living soul was to be seen on the Vaporia, and Mr. Plateas was able to follow the course of his thoughts undisturbed. To tell the truth, his ideas rather lacked sequence, and were much the same thing over and over; but they were so engrossing that he had not quoted a line of Homer all day. If this worry had lasted much longer, it would have effected what all his exercise and sea-bathing had failed to accomplish; the poor man would certainly have been reduced to a shadow.

And still Liakos did not come! For a moment the professor thought of going to look for his friend; bat where should he go? The judge had promised to come, and Florou had been told to get supper for both; Liakos MUST come.

But why didn't he come now? Mr. Plateas paced up and down the Vaporia twenty times at least, and although he kept looking toward his house, there was no sign of the judge. At last! At last he saw his friend coming in the distance.

"Well, is it 'yes' or 'no'?" he cried, as soon as he was near enough to be heard.

"Do let me get my breath first."

From the expression of the poor man's face Mr. Liakos feared that "no" would be more welcome than "yes."

"Can he have repented?" thought the judge; then, taking Mr. Plateas affectionately by the arm, he turned back to prolong the walk, and tried to soothe his friend's amour propre.

"Don't be troubled; she's not a silly girl, but has good sense and good judgment. She will treat your offer as an honor, and will be happy to have a man like you for a husband."

"Never mind about that," said the professor, in a calmer tone. "Tell me how the matter really stands. What have you been doing all this time?"

In relating his story, Mr. Liakos did not tell his friend everything. He passed over the stiffness of Mr. Mitrophanis as well as his cousin's unseemly mirth, and urged so skillfully the need of her good offices as to disarm all objection; he had left the affair in his cousin's charge, and secured her promise to send him word of the result at the professor's house. This was the substance of the conversation; but Mr. Plateas asked so many questions and the judge had to repeat each detail so often, that the sun was setting when the two friends went back to do justice to Florou's supper.

They had scarcely finished when there was a knock at the door, and Florou came in with a note for Mr. Liakos.

Mr. Plateas rose, napkin in hand, and leaned over his friend's chair, eagerly following the words as the judge read aloud:

"MY DEAR COUSIN,--Bring your friend to my house this evening; the young lady will be there. Come early.

YOUR COUSIN."

"What did I tell you!" cried Mr. Liakos, joyfully. "Come, you must get ready."

Mr. Plateas looked very serious; the idea of meeting the young girl made him nervous. What should he say to her? How should he behave? Besides, he was not yet sure of being accepted! Why hadn't the message been a plain "yes" or "no"? The judge had difficulty in persuading Mr. Plateas that the invitation was in itself an assurance of success, and that his cousin and he would do their best to lessen the embarrassment of the meeting. Taking upon himself the duties of valet, Mr. Liakos superintended the poor man's toilet, and having made him look as fine as possible, marched him off.

He would have given almost anything to be well out of the scrape, but it was too late to retreat now.

As they went along, the judge tried in vain to impart some of his own high spirits to his faint-hearted friend. He was brimming over with gladness at the thought of his marriage, which now seemed assured. After so long a separation he was about to see his betrothed, for he felt sure that she would come with her sister. Mr. Plateas had no such reasons for rejoicing. He walked on in silence, paying little heed to his friend's gay sallies; he was trying to think what he should say to the young lady, but nothing came to him.

"By the way," he broke in suddenly, "what is her name?"

"Whose?"

"I mean my future wife. Yesterday I had to let her father see that I didn't even know her name. I mustn't make that mistake to-night!"

At this Mr. Liakos broke into a merry laugh; he was in such high good-humor that he found fun in everything. His companion did not laugh, but repeated:

"What is her name?"

The judge was about to reply when he heard some one coming toward them call out in the darkness:

"Liakos, is that you?"

It was his cousin's husband, who brought word that he was not to be present at the interview. The tactful cousin had felt that it would be better to leave the young lady alone with her suitor; then, too, the younger sister would not come, and the presence of Mr. Liakos was quite unnecessary; her instructions were that he should spend the evening with her husband at the club.

Mr. Plateas felt his knees give way under him. What--go in and face the two ladies all alone! No, decidedly he hadn't the courage for that. But his supporters, one on either side, urged and encouraged the unhappy man until they reached the threshold, when the door opened and they pushed him in, regardless of his protests, then closed it again, and went off to the club.

When Mr. Liakos learned that his sweetheart was not coming, he submitted to his banishment with stoicism; but it seemed to him that the evening at the club would never come to an end. About ten o'clock a servant came to say that Mr. Plateas was waiting for him; he rushed downstairs and found his friend in the street. By the light of a street lamp the judge saw at once from the expression of the suitor's face that the visit had been a complete success. The professor looked like another man.

"Well?" asked Mr. Liakos, eagerly.

"I tell you, she isn't plain at all!" exclaimed Mr. Plateas. "When she speaks her voice is like music, and she has a charming expression! As for her little hand,--it's simply exquisite!"

"You kissed it, I suppose?" said the judge.

"Of course I did!"

"What did you say, and what did she say to you?"

"As though I could tell you everything! The idea!" Then lowering his voice, he added: "Do you know what she said to me? She told me she was glad and grateful that I had asked her to marry me through friendship for you, because such a good friend must make a good husband. I begged her not to say that, else I could not help thinking that she accepted me only out of love for her sister.

"'And why not?' she said gently. 'What sweeter source could the happiness of our future have?'"

Mr. Liakos was touched.

"But really," his friend went on, "I can't begin to tell you everything now. One thing is certain,--I've found a perfect treasure!"

"Did I not tell you so?"

"Yes, but you haven't told me her name, and I didn't dare ask her. What is it?"

The judge bent over and whispered the name that his friend longed to hear.

"There, you know it now."

"Yes, at last!" and the two friends parted,--the one went home with a new joy in his heart, saying over the name he had just learned, while the other softly repeated the name so long dear to him.

A few weeks later, the first Sunday after Easter there was a high festival in the old merchant's house to celebrate the marriage of his two daughters. Of the bridegrooms, Mr. Liakos was not the merrier, for now that his dearest hopes were realized, his soul was filled with a quiet happiness that left no room for words. Mr. Plateas, on the other hand, was overflowing with delight, and his spirits seemed contagious, for all the wedding guests laughed with him. Even His Eminence the Archbishop of Tenos and Syra, who had blessed the double marriage, was jovial with the rest, and showed his learning by wishing the happy couples joy in a line from Homer:

"Thine own wish may the Gods give thee in every place."

To which Mr. Plateas replied majestically:

"The best omen is to battle for one's native land!"

After the wedding, the judge obtained three months' leave, and took his bride for a visit to his old home among his kinsfolk.

How eagerly their return was awaited, and how delighted the sisters were to be together again! The old father trembled with joy.

When the two brothers-in-law were alone, each saw his own happiness reflected in the other's face.

"Well, did I exaggerate when I sang your wife's praises?" asked Mr. Liakos.

"She's a treasure, my dear friend!" cried Mr. Plateas,--"a perfect treasure! In a few months," he went on, "I shall have a new favor to ask of you. I want you to stand as godfather to your nephew."

"What! You too!"

"And you?"

# THE MASSACRE OF THE INNOCENTS
## BY
## MAURICE MAETERLINCK

Towards the hour of supper on Friday, the twenty-sixth day of the month of December, a little shepherd lad came into Nazareth, crying bitterly.

Some peasants, who were drinking ale in the Blue Lion, opened the shutters to look into the village orchard, and saw the child running over the snow. They recognized him as the son of Korneliz, and called from the window: "What is the matter? It's time you were abed!"

But, sobbing still and shaking with terror, the boy cried that the Spaniards had come, that they had set fire to the farm, had hanged his mother among the nut trees and bound his nine little sisters to the trunk of a big tree. At this the peasants rushed out of the inn. Surrounding the child, they stunned him with their questionings and outcries. Between his sobs, he added that the soldiers were on horseback and wore armor, that they had taken away the cattle of his uncle, Petrus Krayer, and would soon be in the forest with the sheep and cows. All now ran to the Golden Swan where, as they knew, Korneliz and his brother-in- law were also drinking their mug of ale. The moment the innkeeper heard these terrifying tidings, he hurried into the village, crying that the Spaniards were at hand.

What a stir, what an uproar there was then in Nazareth! Women opened windows, and peasants hurriedly left their houses carrying lights which were put out when they reached the orchard, where, because of the snow and the full moon, one could see as well as at midday.

Later, they gathered round Korneliz and Krayer, in the open space which faced the inns. Several of them had brought pitchforks and rakes, and consulted together, terror-stricken, under the trees.

But, as they did not know what to do, one of them ran to fetch the cure, who owned Korneliz's farm. He came out of the house with the sacristan carrying the keys of the church. All followed him into the churchyard, whither his cry came to them from the top of the tower, that he beheld nothing either in the fields, or by the forest, but that around the farm he saw ominous red clouds, for all that the sky was of a deep blue and agleam with stars over the rest of the plain.

After taking counsel for a long time in the churchyard, they decided to hide in the wood through which the Spaniards must pass, and, if these were not too numerous, to attack them and recover Petrus Krayer's cattle and the plunder which had been taken from the farm.

Having armed themselves with pitchforks and spades, while the women remained outside the church with the cure, they sought a suitable ambuscade. Approaching a mill on a rising ground adjacent to the verge of the forest, they saw the light of the burning farm flaming against the stars. There they waited under enormous oaks, before a frozen mere.

A shepherd, known as Red Dwarf, climbed the hill to warn the miller, who had stopped his mill when he saw the flames on the horizon. He bade the peasant enter, and both men went to a window to stare out into the night.

Before them the moon shone over the burning farmstead, and in its light they saw a long procession winding athwart the snow. Having carefully scrutinized it, the Dwarf descended where his comrades waited under the trees, and now, they too gradually distinguished four men on horseback behind a flock which moved grazing on the plain.

While the peasants in their blue breeches and red cloaks continued to search about the margins of the mere and under the snowlit trees, the sacristan pointed out to them a box-hedge, behind which they hid.

The Spaniards, driving before them the sheep and the cattle, advanced upon the ice. When the sheep reached the hedge they began to nibble at the green stuff, and now Korneliz broke from the shadows of the bushes, followed by the others with their pitchforks. Then in the midst of the huddled-up sheep and of the cows who stared affrighted, the savage strife was fought out beneath the moon, and ended in a massacre.

When they had slain not only the Spaniards, but also their horses, Korneliz rushed thence across the meadow in the direction of the flames, while the others plundered and stripped the dead. Thereafter all returned to the village with their flocks. The women, who were observing the dark forest from behind the church-yard walls, saw them coming through the trees and ran with the cure to meet them, and all returned dancing joyously amid the laughter of the children and the barking of the dogs.

But, while they made merry, under the pear trees of the orchard, where the Red Dwarf had hung lanterns in honor of the kermesse, they anxiously demanded of the cure what was to be done.

The outcome of this was the harnessing of a horse to a cart in order to fetch the bodies of the woman and the nine little girls to the village. The sisters and other relations of the dead woman got into the cart along with the cure, who, being old and very fat, could not walk so far.

In silence they entered the forest, and emerged upon the moonlit plain. There, in the white light, they descried the dead men, rigid and naked, among the slain horses. Then they moved onward toward the farm, which still burned in the midst of the plain.

When they came to the orchard of the flaming house, they stopped at the gate of the garden, dumb before the overwhelming misfortune of the peasant. For there, his wife hung, quite naked, on the branches of an enormous nut tree, among which he himself was now mounting on a ladder, and beneath which, on the frozen grass, lay his nine little daughters. Korneliz had already, climbed along the vast boughs, when suddenly, by the light of the snow, he saw the crowd who horror-struck watched his every movement. With tears in his eyes, he made a sign to them to help him, whereat the innkeepers of the Blue Lion and the Golden Sun, the cure, with a lantern, and many others, climbed up in the moonshine amid the snow-laden branches, to unfasten the dead. The women of the village received the corpse in their arms at the foot of the tree; even as our Lord Jesus Christ was received by the women at the foot of the Cross.

On the morrow they buried her, and for the week thereafter nothing unusual happened in Nazareth.

But the following Sunday, hungry wolves ran through the village after high mass, and it snowed until midday. Then, suddenly, the sun shone brilliantly, and the peasants went to dine as was their wont, and dressed for the benediction.

There was no one to be seen on the Place, for it froze bitterly. Only the dogs and chickens roamed about under the trees, or the sheep nibbled at a three-cornered bit of grass, while the cure's servant swept away the snow from his garden.

At that moment a troop of armed men crossed the stone bridge at the end of the village, and halted in the orchard. Peasants hurried from their houses, but, recognizing the new-comers as Spaniards, they retreated terrified, and went to the windows to see what would happen.

About thirty soldiers, in full armor, surrounded an old man with a white beard. Behind them, on pillions, rode red and yellow lancers who jumped down and ran over the snow to shake off their stiffness, while several of the soldiers in armor dismounted likewise and fastened their horses to the trees.

Then they moved in the direction of the Golden Sun, and knocked at the door. It was opened reluctantly; the soldiers went in, warmed themselves near the fire, and called for ale.

Presently they came out of the inn, carrying pots, jugs, and rye-bread for their companions, who surrounded the man with the white beard, where he waited behind the hedge of lances.

As the street remained deserted the commander sent some horsemen to the back of the houses, to guard the village on the country side. He then ordered the lancers to bring him all the children of two years old and under, to be massacred, as is written in the Gospel of St. Matthew.

The soldiers first went to the little inn of the Green Cabbage, and to the barber's cottage which stood side by side midway in the street.

One of them opened a sty and a litter of pigs wandered into the village. The innkeeper and the barber came out, and humbly asked the men what they wanted; but they did not understand Flemish, and went into the houses to look for the children.

The innkeeper had one child, who, in its little shift, was screaming on the table where they had just dined. A soldier took it in his arms, and carried it away under the apple trees, while the father and mother followed, crying.

Thereafter the lancers opened other stable doors,--those of the cooper, the blacksmith, the cobbler,--and calves, cows, asses, pigs, goats, and sheep roamed about the square. When they broke the carpenter's windows, several of the oldest and richest inhabitants of the village assembled in the street, and went to meet the Spaniards. Respectfully they took off their caps and hats to the leader in the velvet mantle, and asked him what he was going to do. He did not, understand their language; so some one ran to fetch the cure.

The priest was putting on a gold chasuble in the vestry, in readiness for the benediction. The peasant cried: "The Spaniards are in the orchard!" Horrified, the cure ran to the door of the church, and the choir-boys followed, carrying wax-tapers and censer.

As he stood there, he saw the animals from the pens and stables wandering on the snow and on the grass; the horsemen in the village, the soldiers before the doors, horses tied to trees all along the street; men and women entreating the man who held the child in its little shift.

The cure hastened into the churchyard, and the peasants turned anxiously towards him as he came through the pear trees, like the Divine Presence itself robed in white and gold. They crowded about him where he confronted the man with the white beard.

He spoke in Flemish and in Latin, but the commander merely shrugged his shoulders to show that he did not understand.

The villagers asked their priest in a low voice: "What does he say? What is he going to do?" Others, when they saw the cure in the orchard, came cautiously from their cottages, women hurried up and whispered in groups, while the soldiers, till that moment besieging an inn, ran back at sight of the crowd in the square.

Then the man who held the innkeeper's child by the leg cut off its head with his sword.

The people saw the head fall, and thereafter the body lie bleeding upon the grass. The mother picked it up, and carried it away, but forgot the head. She ran towards her home, but stumbling against a tree fell prone on the snow, where she lay in a swoon, while the father struggled between two soldiers.

Some young peasants cast stones and blocks of wood at the Spaniards, but the horsemen all lowered their lances; the women fled and the cure with his parishioners began to shriek with horror, amid the bleating of the sheep, the cackling of the geese, and the barking of the dogs.

But as the soldiers moved away again into the street, the crowd stood silent to see what would happen.

A troop entered the shop kept by the sacristan's sisters, but came out quietly, without harming the seven women, who knelt on the threshold praying.

From these they went to the inn of St. Nicholas, which belonged to the Hunchback. Here, too, so as to appease them, the door was opened at once; but, when the soldiers reappeared amid a great uproar, they carried three children in their arms. The marauders were surrounded by the Hunchback, his wife, and daughters, all, with clasped hands, imploring for mercy.

When the soldiers came to their white-bearded leader, they placed the children at the foot of an elm, where the little ones remained seated on the snow in their Sunday clothes. But one of them, in a yellow frock, got up and toddled unsteadily towards the sheep. A soldier followed, with bare sword; and the child died with his face in the grass, while the others were killed around the tree.

The peasants and the innkeeper's daughters all fled screaming, and shut themselves up in their houses. The cure, who was left alone in the orchard, threw himself on his knees, first before one horseman, then another, and with crossed arms, supplicated the Spaniards piteously, while the fathers and mothers seated on the snow beyond wept bitterly for the dead children whom they held upon their knees.

As the lancers passed along the street, they noticed a big blue farmstead. When they had tried, in vain, to force open the oaken door studded with nails, they clambered atop of some tubs, which were frozen over near the threshold, and by this means gained the house through the upper windows.

There had been a kermesse in this farm. At sound of the broken window- panes, the families who had assembled there to eat gaufres, custards, and hams, crowded together behind the table on which still stood some empty jugs and dishes. The soldiers entered the kitchen, and after savage struggle in which many were wounded, they seized all the little boys and girls; then, with these, and the servant who had bitten a lancer's thumb, they left the house and fastened the door behind them in such a way that the parents could not get out.

The villagers who had no children slowly left their houses, and followed the soldiers at a distance. They saw them throw down their victims on the grass before the old man, and callously kill them with lance and sword. During this, men and women leaned out of all the windows of the blue house, and out of the barn, blaspheming and flinging their hands to heaven, when they saw the red, pink, and white frocks of their motionless little ones on the grass between the trees. The soldiers next hanged the farm servant at the sign of the Half Moon on the other side of the street, and there was a long silence in the village.

The massacre now became general. Mothers fled from their houses, and attempted to escape through the flower and vegetable gardens, and so into the country beyond, but the horsemen pursued them and drove them back into the street. Peasants with caps in their clasped hands knelt before the men who dragged away their children, while amid the confusion the dogs barked joyously. The cure, with hands upraised to heaven, rushed up and down in front of the houses and under the trees, praying desperately; here and there, soldiers, trembling with cold, blew on their fingers as they moved about the road, or waited with hands in their breeches pockets, and swords under their arms, before the windows of the houses which were being scaled.

Everywhere, as in small bands of twos and threes, they moved along the streets, where these scenes were being enacted, and entered the houses, they beheld the piteous grief of the peasants. The wife of a market- gardener, who occupied a red brick cottage near the church, pursued with a wooden stool the two men who carried off her children in a wheelbarrow. When she saw them die, a horrible sickness came upon her, and they thrust her down on the stool under a tree by the roadside.

Other soldiers swarmed up the lime trees in front of a farmstead with its blank walls tinted mauve, and entered the house by removing the tiles. When they came back on to the roof, the father and mother, with outstretched arms, tried to follow them through the opening, but the soldiers repeatedly pushed them back, and had at last to strike them on the head with their swords, before they could disengage themselves and regain the street.

One family shut up in the cellar of a large cottage lamented near the grating, through which the father wildly brandished a pitchfork. Outside on a heap of manure, a bald old man sobbed all alone; in the square, a woman in a yellow dress had swooned, and her weeping husband now supported her under the arms, against a pear tree; another woman in red fondled her little girl, bereft of her hands, and lifted now one tiny arm, now the other, to see if the child would not move. Yet another woman fled towards the country; but the soldiers pursued her among the hayricks, which stood out in black relief against the fields of snow.

Beneath the inn of the Four Sons of Aymon a surging tumult reigned. The inhabitants had formed a barricade, and the soldiers went round and round the house without being able to enter. Then they were attempting to climb up to the signboard by the creepers, when they noticed a ladder behind the garden door. This they raised against the wall, and went up it in file. But the innkeeper and all his family hurled tables, stools, plates, and cradles down upon them from the windows; the ladder was overturned, and the soldiers fell.

In a wooden hut at the end of the village, another band found a peasant woman washing her children in a tub near the fire. Being old and very deaf, she did not hear them enter. Two men took the tub and carried it away, and the stupefied woman followed with the clothes in which she was about to dress the children. But when she saw traces of blood everywhere in the village, swords in the orchards, cradles overturned in the street, women on their knees, others who wrung their hands over the dead, she began to scream and beat the soldiers, who put down the tub to defend themselves. The cure hastened up also, and with hands clasped over his chasuble, entreated the Spaniards before the naked little ones howling in the water. Some soldiers came up, tied the mad peasant to a tree, and carried off the children.

The butcher, who had hidden his little girl, leaned against his shop, and looked on callously. A lancer and one of the men in armor entered the house and found the child in a copper boiler. Then the butcher in despair took one of his knives and rushed after them into the street, but soldiers who were passing disarmed him and hanged him by the hands to the hooks in the wall--there, among the flayed animals, he kicked and struggled, blaspheming, until the evening.

Near the churchyard, there was a great gathering before a long, low house, painted green. The owner, standing on his threshold, shed bitter tears; as he was very fat and jovial looking, he excited the pity of some soldiers who were seated in the sun against the wall, patting a dog. The one, too, who dragged away his child by the hand, gesticulated as if to say: "What can I do? It's not my fault!"

A peasant who was pursued, jumped into a boat, moored near the stone bridge, and with his wife and children moved away across the unfrozen part of the narrow lagoon. Not daring to follow, the soldiers strode furiously through the reeds. They climbed up into the willows on the banks to try to reach the fugitives with their lances--as they did not succeed, they continued for a long time to threaten the terrified family adrift upon the black water.

The orchard was still full of people, for it was there, in front of the white-bearded man who directed the massacre, that most of the children were killed. Little dots who could just walk alone stood side by side munching their slices of bread and jam, and stared curiously at the slaying of their helpless playmates, or collected round the village fool who played his flute on the grass.

Then suddenly there was a uniform movement in the village. The peasants ran towards the castle which stood on the brown rising ground, at the end of the street. They had seen their seigneur leaning on the battlements of his tower and watching the massacre. Men, women, old people, with hands outstretched, supplicated to him, in his velvet mantle and his gold cap, as to a king in heaven. But he raised his arms and shrugged his shoulders to show his helplessness, and when they implored him more and more persistently, kneeling in the snow, with bared heads, and uttering piteous cries, he turned slowly into the tower and the peasants' last hope was gone.

When all the children were slain, the tired soldiers wiped their swords on the grass, and supped under the pear trees. Then they mounted one behind the other, and rode out of Nazareth across the stone bridge, by which they had come.

The setting of the sun behind the forest made the woods aflame, and dyed the village blood-red. Exhausted with running and entreating, the cure had thrown himself upon the snow, in front of the church, and his servant stood near him. They stared upon the street and the orchard, both thronged with the peasants in their best clothes. Before many thresholds, parents with dead children on their knees bewailed with ever fresh amaze their bitter grief. Others still lamented over the children where they had died, near a barrel, under a barrow, or at the edge of a pool. Others carried away the dead in silence. There were some who began to wash the benches, the stools, the tables, the blood-stained shifts, and to pick up the cradles which had been thrown into the street. Mother by mother moaned under the trees over the dead bodies which lay upon the grass, little mutilated bodies which they recognized by their woollen frocks. Those who were childless moved aimlessly through the square, stopping at times in front of the bereaved, who wailed and sobbed in their sorrow. The men, who no longer wept, sullenly pursued their strayed animals, around which the barking dogs coursed; or, in silence, repaired so far their broken windows and rifled roofs. As the moon solemnly rose through the quietudes of the sky, deep silence as of sleep descended upon the village, where now not the shadow of a living thing stirred.

# SAINT NICHOLAS EVE
## BY
## CAMILLE LEMONNIER

## I.

T his is the finest day of the year, Nelle," exclaimed a big stalwart man of about sixty, with a bright smile, to a fresh clean-looking woman, who at that moment came down the ladder of the boat with shavings in her hand.

"Yes, Tobias," replied the woman, "it is indeed the day of days for boatmen."

"Do you remember the first feast of St. Nicholas, which we kept together, after we were married?"

"Yes, Tobias, it will soon be forty years ago."

"Hendrik Shippe, our master, came on to the boat and said to me: 'Tobias, my lad, you must keep the festival of our blessed saint in a proper way, now that you have brought a wife to your boat.' With that, he put a five-franc piece into my hand. 'Mynheer Shippe,' I replied, 'I am more pleased with your five-franc piece than if I had been crowned.' I went out without saying anything to my dear Nelle, crossed the plank, and ran into the village to buy cream, eggs, flour, apples, and coffee. Who was glad when I came back with all the good things and laid them side by side on the table, while the fire burned brightly in the stove? Who was glad? Tell me, my Nelle."

"Ah, Tobias! We sat hand in hand that evening till ten o'clock as we had sat together in the moonlight on the banks of the Scheldt before we were married. But we did other things, too, on that day, lots of other things. What did we do? Do you remember, Tobias?"

"Oh! oh! we made golden apple pancakes; I can smell them now. I wanted you to teach me how to toss them, but I tossed two into the fire, and the third fell into the cat's mouth. Yes, yes, Nelle, I remember."

"Now, my man, we must make apple pancakes again in memory of that happy evening; I have brought shavings to light the fire. One day, Riekje and Dolf will recall the good festival of Saint Nicholas as we now recall it."

It was thus that the boatman, Tobias Jeffers, spoke to his wife Nelle, on board the Guldenvisch.

The Guldenvisch, which had been thus named from the pretty gold-fish which shone afore and aft on her prows, was Hendrik Shippe's best boat, and he had entrusted it to the care of Tobias Jeffers, his ablest boatman. There was not a smarter looking craft in Termonde, nor one better fitted for hard work. It was a pleasure to watch her glide along, her waist well under water, laden with corn, wood, straw, or provisions; to see, too, her big brown hull set off with red and blue lines, her prows ornamented with the long smooth-scaled gold-fish, her shining bridge and her little cloud of smoke curling out of the black painted funnel.

That day, the Guldenvisch, like all the other boats on the Scheldt, had stopped work. She was anchored to a strong rope, and toward seven in the evening there was nothing to be seen but the light on the top of the funnel, and the port-holes, round and bright as cod's eyes.

Preparations for the feast of St. Nicholas were in full swing in the little room under the bridge; two candles burned in the brass candle- sticks, and the stove roared like water which rushes from a lock when the gates are opened.

The good Nelle pushed the door and Tobias went in quietly, thinking of the happy days which he had just recalled.

"Maman Nelle," said a young voice, "I can see the round windows lighting up everywhere one after the other on the dark water."

"Yes, Riekje," Nelle replied, "but it is not to see the windows lighted up on the water that you stay near the window, but to see if that fine lad, Dolf, is not coming back to the boat."

Riekje laughed.

"Maman Nelle sees straight into my heart," said she, sitting down near the fire, and stitching away at a baby's cap, which she held in her hand.

"Who could not see straight into the heart of a woman who is in love with her husband, Riekje?" asked old Nelle.

As she spoke she took off the top of the stove and put the pot on the fire, much to its delight, for it began to hiss like the rocket sent off from the market-place the day before in honor of the election of a new mayor. Then Nelle wetted her finger and snuffed the candles, and the flame which had been flickering unsteadily at the end of the black wick burned brightly again and lit up the little room with a beautiful quiet light.

The room was very small and was something like a big cask cut in half, with its curved wooden ceiling, and its stave-like wooden panels. A coating of shiny, brown tar covered the walls; in places, especially over the stove, it was black as ebony. The furniture consisted of a table, two chairs, a chest which served as a bed, and near the chest a white wooden box with two shelves. On these two shelves lay linen, caps, handkerchiefs, women's dresses, and men's jackets, all smelling somewhat of fish. In one corner hung the nets, together with tarred capes, boots, oilskin hats, and enormous sheepskin gloves. Strings of onions encircled a picture of the Virgin, and some twenty dried herrings with shining bellies were strung by their gills on a thread under an enameled clock.

All this could be seen by the light of the two candles, whose flicker made the shadows dance on the ceiling; but the fairest thing to see was beautiful dark Riekje sitting near the fire. She had broad shoulders, a plump neck, and strong arms; her cheeks were round and sunburnt, her eyes of a dusky brown, her lips full and red; and as for her black hair, which was coiled six times round her head, the coils were heavy as the towing ropes used on the banks of the river. Though so gentle and quiet, she was often lost in sombre fancies; but when Dolf was near, her face lit up with smiles and her teeth were bright as a wet oar's blade shining in the sun. Then she no longer gloomed; the cloud which veiled sad memories was lifted, bright hopes irradiated her face, every line in which sparkled like whitebait in the meshes of a net. Then it was that she would turn to her "beau garcon" and clap her hands. The flame which escaped through the stove door caught her cheeks at that moment, and they were red as salmon; the dark eyes fixed on her work were bright as living coal. Yet two other things shone like her eyes; the pendant hanging to the gold ring in her ear, and the silver ring which she wore on her finger.

"Are you comfortable, Riekje?" asked Nelle, from time to time. "Do your straw-lined sabots keep your feet warm?"

"Yes, maman Nelle, I am as happy as a queen," she answered, smiling.

"As a queen, you say," replied Nelle. "You will be like a queen, soon, my girl, for you are going to eat some of my apple keikebakken. There comes Dolf over the planks, bringing us flour, eggs, and cream; you will have something to say about my pancakes, Riekje."

She opened the door, for a heavy step could be heard on the bridge of the boat.

# II.

As a broad-shouldered man, with a frank, smiling face, stepped into the cheerful light of the room, his head almost touched the ceiling.

"There you are, mother!" he cried.

He threw his hat into a corner and began to empty his pockets with great care, placing the paper bags on the table.

"Dolf, I was sure you'd do it; you've forgotten the pint of milk," cried maman Nelle when everything was spread out.

Dolf drew back, and made a grimace as if he really would have to go back to the shop. But, at the same time, he winked to Riekje to let her know that it was a joke. Nelle, who had not seen this, struck the palm of her left hand with her right fist, complaining bitterly.

"What are we to do without milk, Dolf? I must go to town myself. These big lads think of nothing but their love, Tobias."

"If I produced the milk from under Riekje's chair, would you kiss me, mother?" Dolf broke in, heartily laughing, and throwing one arm round his mother's neck, while he held the other hidden behind his back.

"Be quiet, bad boy," said Nelle, half in anger, half jokingly; "how can there be any milk under Riekje's chair?"

"Will you kiss me?" he replied blithely. "Once--twice---"

Nelle turned quickly to Riekje:

"Get up, my girl, so that I may see whether I am to kiss your good-for- nothing husband."

Dolf bent over Riekje and looked under her chair, pretending not to find anything at first; finally he held the jug of milk triumphantly out at arm's length. He laughed gayly, his hand on his thigh:

"Ah! who'll be kissed now, mother? Who'll be kissed?"

They all roared with laughter at the good joke.

"Dolf, kiss Riekje; bees like honey," cried Nelle.

Her lover made a ceremonious bow to Riekje, placed one foot behind the other, pressed his hand to his heart, as the quality do, and, with a solemn air, exclaimed:

"Soul of my soul, may I embrace one so fair as you?"

Then, without waiting for a reply, Dolf threw his arm round Riekje's waist, raised her from her chair, and pressed his young lips upon her neck. But Riekje half turned her head, and they kissed one another warmly on the lips.

"Riekje," said Dolf, licking his lips in a greedy fashion, "a kiss like that is better than ryspap."

"Nelle, let us do the same thing," said Tobias. "I delight to see them so happy."

"Willingly," said Nelle. "Were we not the same in our own kissing days?"

"Ah! Nelle, they are always kissing days when there are two, and when there is some little spot on earth where they can make a peaceful home."

Tobias kissed his wife's cheeks; then, in her turn, Nelle gave him two big kisses which resounded like the snapping of dry firewood.

"Riekje," Dolf whispered, "I shall always love you."

"Dolf," replied Riekje, "I shall love you till death."

"I am two years older than you are, Riekje. When you were ten I was twelve, and I think I loved you then, but not so much as now."

"No, dear, you have only known me since last May. All the rest is not true. Tell me, Dolf, that all the rest is not true. I must hear it, that I may love you without any feeling of shame." As Riekje leaned against her husband's breast, she threw herself back a little, and it was evident that she would soon be a mother.

"Come, children," cried maman Nelle, "it's time now to make the batter."

She reached down an iron pan, lined with shining white enamel, poured in the flour, the eggs, and the milk. After turning up her sleeves over her brown arms, she whipped all vigorously together. When she had beaten the batter well, she placed the pan on a chair near the fire and covered it with a cloth that it might rise. Tobias took down the frying-pan, greased it with a little lard, and put it on the stove for a moment to warm, so that the batter might brown all over equally.

Riekje and Dolf, sitting side by side on the same bench, took some apples from a basket, cored, and afterwards sliced them. Then Nelle went slyly to fetch a second saucepan from the cupboard and placed it on the fire; she poured in some warm water, adding flour, thyme, and laurel leaves. Dolf noticed that the saucepan contained something else, but Nelle covered it up so quickly that he could not tell whether it were meat or cabbage. He was puzzled and tried to guess.

Gradually the contents began to boil, and a thin, brown smoke escaped from the lid which bubbled up and down. Dolf stretched his nose towards the stove and opened his nostrils wide enough for a nut to rest in each, but still he could not define the smell.

When maman Nelle went to lift the lid to see if the contents were cooking properly, he stood on tip-toe behind her back, making himself, for the fun of the thing, first quite short, and then quite tall.

Riekje laughed quietly as she looked out of the corner of her eye. Suddenly Dolf gave a cry to surprise his mother, but Nelle had seen him come up, and just at the moment when he thought to look into the pot she put down the lid and nodded to him:

"Who's caught now, Dolf?" But he cried out, laughing; "I saw that time, mother. It's Slipper's old cat that you have put into the stew-pan, with some candle-grease."

"Yes," replied Nelle, "and next time I shall fry mice. Go and set the table, and leave me alone you bad fellow."

Dolf went quietly into the closet, leading from the cabin. Choosing a very white and well-starched shirt he put it on over his clothes and came back flapping the tails.

When Nelle saw him she put her hands to her hips and laughed till the tears streamed down her face; Riekje clapped her hands and laughed too. Tobias remained serious, and, while Dolf walked up and down the room, asking Nelle if she would not have him for a cook, he took the plates out of the cupboard and began to rub them on a corner of the shirt. Then the good Nelle fell into a chair and slapped her knee with her hand as she rocked herself backwards and forwards. At last the table was spread; the plates shone round and bright as the moon in water, while the pewter forks beside them were bright as silver.

Nelle opened the saucepan for the last time, tasted the gravy, and raising the big tin spoon, in command, cried:

"Come to table. Now you can enjoy yourselves."

They moved the big chest up to the table, for there were two chairs only, and Dolf sat on it near Riekje. Tobias took a chair, placed another beside him for Nelle, stretched out his legs and crossed his hands over his stomach. Then a cloud of smoke rose up to the wooden roof and the saucepan appeared on the table, making a sound like the melting of snow in the sun.

"It's Slipper's cat, I knew it was," cried Dolf, when Nelle had taken off the lid.

Each held out his plate and Nelle, looking into the pot, produced some brown meat, cut into pieces, which she poured on to the plates with plenty of gravy. Dolf looked carefully at the pieces which Nelle gave him, smelt them, and after a moment's pause, brought his fist down on the table and cried:

"God forgive me, Riekje, it's scheisels."

It was indeed ox tripe prepared in the Flemish manner, with liver, heart and lungs. Dolf put his fork into the biggest pieces first, and as he swallowed them, rubbed his hands over his stomach to show his approval.

"Nelle is a capital cook," said Tobias. "I know King Leopold eats scheisels cooked in wine, but Nelle makes them just as good with water."

"This is indeed a fine Saint Nicholas we are keeping," said Dolf to his wife, smacking his tongue against the roof of his mouth. "We shall always remember eating tripe on St. Nicholas day this year."

Nelle now got up and pushed the frying-pan on the fire. She took care first to rake out the ashes and to put some fagots of wood on the flames. When the stove began to roar again Nelle became serious and uncovered her batter.

It had risen to the top of the pan, and was rich, thick, and fragrant, with here and there little bubbles on its surface. Nelle plunged a big spoon into the beautiful, deep mass, and when she drew it out long threads hung from it on all sides. The frying-pan hissed and bubbled as the batter was poured on to the brown butter around the slices of apple which Nelle had carefully laid in first. When the pancake began to brown at the edges it was tossed into the air by a clever twist of the arm. Dolf and Tobias clapped their hands and Riekje admired Nelle's dexterity.

"A plate, quick!" The first koekebakke was spread out, golden and juicy, the color of a fried sole. Who would have this first one? It should be for Tobias; Tobias passed it on to Riekje, and the young girl cut it in pieces and shared it with Dolf.

Tobias watched them both eat it with pleasure, then said to Nelle: "Ah! my wife, I see that the koekebakken are as good as when you made them for me the first time."

In gratitude for these kindly words a big juicy pancake, round as a quoit, fell on to his plate. "The sun shines on my plate just as I see it shine on the water from the bridge," he cried out.

More batter was quickly poured into the frying-pan, the butter bubbled, the fire roared, and round pancakes fell on the table as tench.

"Now it's my turn, mother," cried Dolf, when the bowl was almost empty.

Nelle sat down near Tobias and ate the two pancakes which she had kept for herself, because they were not quite so perfect as the others. Dolf poured the batter into the frying-pan, but not in a ring, as Nelle did, for his idea was to make a mannikin such as are to be seen in the bakers' shop windows on the eve of St. Nicholas. The body and head were soon visible; then came the arms and legs. Dolf, leaning over his work, carefully guided the spoon, for fear of pouring the mixture too quickly or too slowly. Suddenly he uttered a proud cry and slid the absurd figure on to Riekje's plate, but no sooner did it touch the earthenware than it broke in two, and ran into an indistinguishable mass. He tried again and again, until the mannikin could stand on its legs. Then he gave him a slice of apple for a head, to make him look more natural.

"My lad," Tobias said to his son, "in the corner among the shavings you will find an old bottle of schiedam which I brought from Holland, along with three others; they have been drunk, there is only this one left. Bring it here."

Dolf obeyed, and Nelle took out some small glasses. Tobias uncorked the bottle, and filled two of them, one for himself and one for Dolf. Anyone could see that it was good old schiedam, for Tobias and his son nodded their heads and smacked their lips with pleasure.

"Ah! my daughter," said Nelle, "it will be a happy day for us all in two years' time, when a little sabot stands in the hearth filled with carrots and turnips."

"Yes, Riekje, it will be a happy day for us all," said Dolf, closing his big hands over hers.

Riekje raised her eyes, in which stood a tear, and said softly:

"Dolf, it's a good heart you have."

He sat down beside her and threw his arm round her waist:

"I am neither good nor bad, my Riekje, but I love you with all my heart."

Riekje kissed him.

"Dolf dear, when I think of the past I hardly know how I can still care for life."

"The past is past, my beloved Riekje," replied Dolf.

"Ah! Dolf, dear Dolf, there are times when I think it would almost be better to be up there now, so that I might tell the good Virgin all you have done for me."

"Riekje, I am sad when you are sad: you do not wish to make me unhappy about you this evening?"

"No, Dolf dear, I would give my life to save you one moment's pain."

"Then show me your beautiful white teeth, Riekje, and turn round and smile at me."

"As you will, my Dolf, for all my joys and sorrows are yours. I have only you in the world."

"Since that is so, Riekje, I wish to be everything to you; your father, your husband, and your child. Tell me, Riekje, I am your baby, am I not? There will be two of us to love our mother."

Riekje took Dolf's head in her hands, and kissed his cheeks; she paused from time to time as one pauses when drinking sweet liqueur to enjoy the flavor, and then drinks again. Then she put her lips to his ear and whispered:

"Dolf, my darling Dolf, will you love it?"

Dolf raised his hand solemnly.

"I call God to witness, Riekje, I shall love it as if it were my own flesh and blood."

"Our lad has been lucky," said Nelle to her husband. "Riekje is a dear lass. She brought joy with her when she entered our house, Tobias."

"We are very poor, Nelle," he replied, "but old parents like ourselves can have no greater happiness than to see their children sitting round their fire in love with one another."

"They love one another as we loved, Tobias."

"You were then a pretty, fresh girl from Deurne, Nelle, with cheeks as red as a cherry and a nose like a pretty little seashell. When you went to church on Sunday with your fine winged cape and your big metal star, which all young girls wear, every man turned to look at you."

"But I did not look at them, for Tobias was my sweetheart; a fine lad he was, with black hair and a pointed beard, a green velvet jacket, bright eyes and big brown cheeks."

"Ah! Nelle, how happy we were in those days when we could clasp hands behind a hedge, and sometimes, too, I stole a kiss when your head was turned away."

"That's true, Tobias, but afterwards, I did not turn my head away and you kissed me all the same."

"There is no greater happiness on earth, my Dolf," said Riekje, "than to grow old loving one another; the years don't then gloom as life lengthens, and when one dies, the other soon follows."

"It is so, Riekje. If my old father dies first, I shall say to the gravedigger, 'Dig a big hole, sexton, for my mother will lie there too.'"

"Ah! heart of me!" cried Riekje, clasping her husband in her arms, "I shall say the same thing to the sexton if you die first, my Dolf."

The fire roared in the stove, and the candles, which were nearly burned down, gave a flickering light. Nelle had forgotten to snuff the wicks and the thieves which fell into the tallow made it drop in big yellow tears. In the ruddy light, which widened in circles like water where a stone has fallen, the little narrow cabin seemed a paradise because of the happy hearts which were in it.

The rough head of the old man, with his prominent cheek-bones, his gray beard, his shaven lips, and ears pierced with gold rings, stood out the color of smoked salmon, against the brown wall. Near him sat Nelle. Her back was turned to the candles, and now and again, when she moved her head, a bright light caught her brow, the gold rings sparkled in her ears, the tip of her nose shone, and the wings of her cap stood out in the shadow like the wings of a bird. She wore a coarse woollen skirt, over which hung the full basque of her flowered jacket, but as Tobias' arm was round her waist the stiff pleats were not in such perfect order as usual.

Riekje and Dolf sat hand in hand on the other side of the room; they had drawn as idea little that they might look at one another unbeknown to the others, and their faces were close together. When they moved, the candlelight struck Dolf's shaven chin, Riekje's red lips, their necks or their pierced ears, as the sun strikes the belly of a fish below the water. Kettles, saucepans, and pots shone on the shelves and the shadows in the corners were soft as velvet.

"What is the matter, Riekje?" cried Dolf suddenly, "you are as white as those plates in the cupboard, and your eyes are closed. My Riekje, what is the matter with you?"

"Ah! Dolf," replied Riekje, "if it were to happen to-day! I have been in pain all the afternoon, and now I feel worse. My child! If I die, you will love it, Dolf, dear?"

"Mother! Mother!" cried Dolf, "I am sick at heart."

Then he hid his face in his big hands and began to sob, without knowing the reason.

"Come, Dolf, be brave," said Tobias, tapping him on the shoulder. "We have all gone through this!"

"Riekje, Riekje, my heart!" said Nelle in tears, "no greater happiness could come to us on Saint Nicholas day. Poor folk rejoice more over a child that is born to them, than over all the treasures in the world, but the child whom God sends on Easter Day or St. Nicholas day is above all welcome."

"Dolf, you can run better than I can," said Tobias. "Run and fetch Madame Puzzel; we will look after Riekje."

Then Dolf pressed Riekje once more to his heart, and ran up the ladder. The plank which connected the boat with the shore shook as he crossed it.

"He is already a long way off," said Tobias.

# III.

The night hung over the town like a great bird, but it had snowed on the preceding days, and through the darkness Dolf could see the blanched face of the earth, white as the face of the dead. He ran full speed along the river bank as one pursued by the tide, though, even then, his footfall was not so rapid as the beating of his heart. The distant lights through the fog seemed to him like a procession of taper-bearers at a funeral; he did not know how this idea arose, but it terrified him, for behind it again he saw death. Then he came upon silent figures hastening mysteriously along.

"Doubtless, they have been suddenly called to the bedside of the dying," he muttered.

It was now he remembered that it is customary in Flanders on that night to replace the hay, carrots, and turnips which the little ones put on the hearth to feed Saint Nicholas' ass, by big dolls, wooden horses, musical instruments, violins, or simply by mannikins in spikelaus, according as each can afford.

"Ah," he said to himself, comforted, "they are fathers and mothers going to the shops." But now the gloomy lights which resembled the taper- bearers seemed to be chasing one another along the quays; their little flames ran in every direction, crossed one another, and looked like big fireflies. "I must see double," he said, "the fireflies can be in my brain only."

Suddenly he heard voices, calling, crying out, lamenting.

Torches moved to and fro on the river bank, their red tongues of flame blown by the wind amid clouds of smoke. In the uncertain light he could at last distinguish figures rushing about, others leaning over the river, black as well. This explained everything: the lamps had not moved, but he had been misled by the flitting torches.

"Let us fetch Dolf Jeffers," cried two men. "No one else will be able to do it."

"Here is Dolf Jeffers," cried the good fellow at that moment, "what do you want?"

He recognized the men; they were his friends, his fellow-workers, boatmen, like himself. All surrounded him, gesticulating. An old man, wizened as a dried plaice, tapped him on the shoulder, and said:

"Dolf, for God's sake! A fellow-creature is being drowned. Help! Perhaps it's already too late. Strip off your clothes, Dolf."

Dolf looked at the water, the lanterns, the night above him, and the men who urged him on.

"Comrades," he cried, "before God, I cannot. Riekje is in labor and my life is not my own."

"Dolf! Help!" cried the old man again, as with trembling hands he pointed to his dripping clothes. "I have three children, Dolf, yet I have been in twice. I have no strength left."

Dolf turned to the pale faces which stood in a circle round him.

"Cowards," he cried. "Is there not one among you who will save a drowning man?"

The greater number bent their heads and shrugged their shoulders, feeling that they had deserved the reproach.

"Dolf," the old man cried, "as sure's death's death, I shall try again, if you do not go."

"God! God! There he is!" cried the men at that moment, who were moving the torches over the water. "We saw his head and feet. Help!"

Dolf threw off his coat and said to the boatmen coldly: "I will go."

Then he spoke again: "One of you run to Madame Puzzel and take her back to the Guldenvisch at once."

He made the sign of the cross and muttered between his teeth: "Jesus Christ, who died on the cross to save sinners, have mercy on me."

He went down the bank, with bared breast, and the crowd who followed him trembled for his life. He looked for a moment at the traitorous river, on which the torches dripped tears of blood, as if he saw death before him. The flood gurgled, as when a great fish strikes the water with its tail.

"There he is," the same voices cried.

Then the abyss was opened.

"Riekje!" cried Dolf.

The cold river closed about him like a prison. Increasing circles were all that ruffled that black surface, which seemed blacker than ever by the light of the torches.

Absolute silence reigned among the men who looked on from the bank. Some stood up to their waist in water, feeling about with long poles; others unfastened ropes, which they sent adrift; three men slipped into a boat and rowed noiselessly, moving their lanterns carefully over the surface of the water. Beneath all was the gentle murmur of the cruel Scheldt as, lapping the banks, it flowed eternally onward.

Twice Dolf came to the surface and twice he disappeared again. They could see his arms move and his face seemed paler in the darkness. Once more he clove the icy gulf and plunged still deeper. Suddenly his legs became motionless, as if entangled in the treacherous sea-weed by the spiteful water-spirits. The drowning man had seized him, and Dolf realized that if he could not get free, both would be lost. His limbs were more tightly pressed than in a vice. Then there was a terrible struggle, and the men both sank to the mud of the river-bed. In the drowning darkness they fought, bit, tore one another, like mortal enemies. Dolf at last gained the upper hand; the paralyzing arms ceased to strangle him, and he felt an inert mass floating upon him. A terrible lassitude as of a sleep overcame him, his head fell forward, the water entered his mouth. But the light of the torches penetrated the dark water; he gathered up his strength and dragged after him the prey which he had robbed from the hungry eels. Then at last he breathed pure air again.

With that there was a great outburst from the bank.

"Courage, Dolf," cried the breathless crowd, stretching out over the river. One or two boat-men had piled some wood and set light to it. The flames rose spirally and lit up the sky for some distance.

"This way, Dolf! Courage, Dolf! A brave heart, courage!" yelled the crowd.

Dolf was just about to reach the bank: he parted the water with all his remaining strength and pushed the limp body before him. The red light from the wood-fire spread over his hands and face like burning oil, and suddenly it caught the face of the drowning man, by his side.

No sooner did he see that pale face than, uttering a cry of rage, he pushed it to the bottom of the water. He had recognized the man who had dishonored Riekje. Dolf, a right loyal fellow, had had pity on the poor lonely fisher lass and had made her his wife before God and man. He pushed him from him, but the drowning man, who felt the water close once more about him, clung to his saviour with an iron grasp. Then both disappeared in the darkness of death.

Dolf heard a voice say within himself:

"Die, Jacques Karnavash; there is not room in the world for you and Riekje's child."

To this another voice replied:

"Live, Jacques Karnavash, for it would be better to strike your mother dead."

# IV.

"There's Dolf bringing Madame Puzzel back with him," said Nelle, after about an hour.

The gangway swung under the weight of two people and sabots sounded on the bridge, while a voice cried:

"Tobias! Tobias! get the lantern and light Madame Puzzel."

Tobias took one of the candles and carefully sheltered it with his hand as he opened the door.

"This way," he cried, holding it ajar. "This way!"

The midwife stepped down the ladder, and a man followed her.

"Ah! Madame Puzzel, Riekje will be pleased to see you. Come in," said Tobias. "Good-evening, lad. Oh! it's Lucas."

"Good evening, Tobias," said the young man. "Dolf has stayed behind with his comrades, so I brought Madame Puzzel."

"Come and have a drink, my son, then you can go back to Dolf."

Nelle now came forward.

"Good-evening, Madame Puzzel, how are you? Here is a chair. Sit down and warm yourself."

"Good-evening to you all," replied the fat little old woman. "So we are going to have christening sugar on board the Guldenvisch this evening. It's your first, is it not, Riekje? Come, Nelle, make me some coffee and give me some supper."

"Riekje," said the young boatman, "I brought Madame Puzzel because Dolf was dragged off by his comrades. He must not see you suffer. It is better not, so the others have carried him off to have a drink to give him courage."

"I shall be braver, too, if he is not here," replied Riekje, raising her eyes full of tears.

"Yes," said Nelle, in her turn," it's better for every one that Dolf should not be here."

Tobias then poured out a glass of gin and gave it to the man, saying:

"There's something for your trouble, Lucas. When you have drunk that, your legs will lengthen like a pair of oars, and you'll get back to your friends in no time."

Lucas drank it off at two gulps. As he drank the first he said to the company:

"Here's to every one's health."

He drank the second, saying to himself:

"To Dolf's health, if he is still alive."

Then he said good-evening. As the lad left the cabin, the kettle was singing on the fire and there was a good smell of coffee in the room, for Nelle with the mill on her lap was crushing the black berries, which snapped cheerily.

Madame Puzzel had unfastened the metal clasp of her big black-hooded cloak and taken her spectacle case and knitting from her basket. She put on her spectacles, took up her knitting, sat down by the fire and began to knit. She wore a woollen flowered jacket under a black shawl, and a skirt of linsey-woolsey. From time to time she looked over her spectacles without raising her head and glanced at Riekje walking up and down the room groaning. When the pain became worse, Madame Puzzel tapped her on the cheek, and said:

"Be brave, Riekje. You cannot think what a joy it is to hear the little one cry for the first time. It is like eating vanilla cream in Paradise listening to beautiful violin music."

Tobias, having put back the big chest which served as a bed against the wall, went to fetch two sea-weed mattresses from his own bed, and, as he laid them on the chest, there was a healthy salt smell in the room. Then Nelle covered the mattresses with spotless coarse linen sheets, and smoothed them with the palm of her hand to take out the creases and make it as soft as a feather-bed. Towards midnight, Madame Puzzel folded up her knitting, placed her spectacles on the table, crossed her arms and looked into the fire; then she began to prepare the linen, made a hole in the pillows and looked at the time by the big silver watch which she wore under her jacket. Finally, she yawned six consecutive times and went to sleep with one eye open.

Riekje wrung her hands and cried out:

"Mamae Puzzel! Mamae Puzzel!"

"Mama Puzzel can do nothing for you, Riekje," replied the midwife. "You must be patient."

Within the room, the kettle sang on the fire; without, the water lapped against the boat. Voices died away along the banks, and doors were shut.

"It is midnight," said Tobias, "those are the people leaving the inn."

"Ah! Dolf! dear Dolf!" cried Riekje, each time. "Why does he not come back?"

"I see the lamps in the houses and boats being put out one by one. Dolf will be in directly," said Nelle to quiet her. But Dolf did not return.

Two hours after midnight Riekje was in such pain that she had to go to bed. Madame Puzzel sat beside her and Nelle told her beads. Two hours passed thus.

"Dolf! Dolf!" Riekje cried incessantly. "Why does he stay away so long when his Riekje is dying?"

Tobias went up the ladder now and again to see if Dolf were not coming back. The little port-hole of the Guldenvisch reflected its red light on the dark water; there was no other window alight in the town. In the distance a church clock rang out the quarters, the chimes falling through the night like a flight of birds escaped from a cage. Tobias listened to the notes of the music which spoke of the son whom he awaited. Gradually the lights were relit one after another in the houses, and lamps twinkled like stars along the water's edge. A fresh cold dawn broke over the town. Then a little child began to cry in the boat, and it seemed to those who heard it sweet as the bleating of a lambkin.

"Riekje! Riekje!"

A distant voice called Riekje. It was Dolf who sprang over the bridge and rushed into the room. Riekje, who was asleep, opened her eyes and saw her loving lad kneeling beside her. Tobias threw his cap up in the air, and Nelle, laughing, pinched the face of the new-born babe whom Madame Puzzel swaddled on her knee. When the baby was well wrapped up, Madame Puzzel placed it in Dolf's arms and he kissed it cautiously with little smacks.

Riekje called Dolf to her side, took his head in her hand, and fell asleep until morning. Dolf put his head beside her on the pillow, and their breath and their hearts were as one during that sleep.

# V.

Dolf went off into the town one morning.

Funeral bells were tolling, and their knell echoed through the air like the hoarse cry of gulls and petrels above the shipwrecked.

A long procession disappeared through the church porch, and the altar draped in black shone with its many wax lights, which glistened as the tears in a widow's eyes.

"Who has died in the town?" Dolf asked of an old beggar sitting at the threshold of the church, his chin on his knees. "The son of a rich family, a man of property, Jacques Karnavash. Give a trifle for the repose of his soul."

Dolf took off his hat and entered the church.

He hid himself behind a pillar and saw the silver-nailed coffin disappear beneath the black catafalque.

"Lord God," he said, "may Thy will be done. Forgive him as I have forgiven him."

When the crowd made their taper-offering, he took a wax light from the chorister and followed those who walked round the branch candlesticks mighty as trees, which burned at the four corners of the pall.

Then he knelt down in the dark corner, far from the men and women who had come out of respect for the dead, and these words were mingled with his prayer:

"God, Father of men, forgive me also; I saved this man from drowning, but my courage failed when I first saw that it was my Riekje's seducer, and I desired vengeance. Then I pushed from me the man who had a mother, and whom I was to restore to that mother; I thrust him back under the water, before I saved him. Forgive me, O Lord, and if I must be punished for this, punish me only."

Then he left the church and thought deep down in his heart:

"Now there is no one living who can say that Riekje's child is not my child."

"Hey! Dolf," voices called to him from the quay.

He recognized those who had seen him bring Jacques Karnavash to the bank.

Their rude hearts had trembled for him like women's hearts; they had clung to him and said:

"Dolf, you are worth all of us put together."

Suddenly he had fallen on the pavement, but they had carried him near the kitchen fire of an inn, had revived him with gin and looked after him until he felt strong enough to run back to his beloved Riekje.

"Dolf," they now cried.

And when Dolf turned, the old boatman clasped him in his arms and said:

"My dear son, I love you as if you were my own flesh and blood."

The others pressed his hand heartily, saying:

"Dolf, we shall at least have known one really brave fellow before we die."

"As for me, comrades," said Dolf, laughing, "I shall not die before I drink a glass with you to the health of the fine little chap Riekje gave me the other night."

# IN LOVE WITH THE CZARINA
## BY
## MAURICE JOKAI

I n the time of the Czar Peter III. a secret society existed at St. Petersburg which bore the title of "The Nameless." Its members used to assemble in the house of a Russian nobleman, Jelagin by name, who alone knew the personality of each visitor, they being, for the most part, unknown to one another. Distinguished men, princes, ladies of the court, officers of the Guard, Cossack soldiers, young commercial men, musicians, street-singers, actors and actresses, scientific men, clergymen and statesmen, used to meet here. Beauty and talent were alone qualifications for entry into the Society, the members of which were selected by Jelagin. Every one addressed the other as "thee" and "thou," and they only made use of Christian names such as Anne, Alexandra. Katharine, Olga, Peter, Alexis, and Ivan. And for what purpose did they assemble here? To amuse themselves at their ease. Those who, by the prejudices of caste and rank, were utterly severed, and who occupied the mutual position of master and slave, tore the chains of their barriers asunder, and all met here. It is quite possible that he with whom the grenadier-private is now playing chess is the very same general who might order him a hundred lashes to-morrow, should he take a step on parade without his command! And now he contends with him to make a queen out of a pawn!

It is also probable that the pretty woman who is singing sportive French songs to the accompaniment of the instrument she strikes with her left hand is one of the Court ladies of the Czarina, who, as a rule, throws half-roubles out of her carriage to the street-musicians! Perhaps she is a Princess? possibly the wife of the Lord Chamberlain? or even higher in grade than this? Russian society, both high and low, flower and root, met in Jelagin's castle, and while there enjoyed equality in the widest sense of the word. Strange phenomenon! That this should take place in Russia, where so much is thought of aristocratic rank, official garb, and exterior pomp; where an inferior is bound to dismount from his horse upon meeting a superior, where sub-officers take off their coats in token of salute when they meet those of higher rank, and where generals kiss the priest's hands and the highest aristocrats fall on their faces before the Czar! Here they sing and dance and joke together, make fun of the Government, and tell anecdotes of the High Priests, utterly fearless, and dispensing with salutations!

Can this be done for love of novelty? The existence of this secret society was repeatedly divulged to the police, and these cannot be reproached for not having taken the necessary steps to denounce it; but proceedings once begun usually evaporated into thin air, and led to no results. The investigating officer either never discovered suspicious facts, or, if he did, matters were adjourned. Those who were arrested in connection with the affair were in some way set at liberty in peace and quietness; every document relating to the matter was either burned or vanished, and whole sealed cases of writings were turned into plain white paper. When an influential officer took energetically in hand the prosecution of "The Nameless," he was generally sent to a foreign country on an important mission, from which he did not return for a considerable period. "The Nameless Society" must have had very powerful protectors. At the conclusion of one of these free and easy entertainments, a young Cossack hetman remained behind the crowd of departing guests, and when quite alone with the host he said to him:

"Jelagin, did you see the pretty woman with whom I danced the mazurka to-night?"

"Yes, I saw her. Are you smitten with her, as others have been?"

"That woman I must make my wife."

Jelagin gave the Cossack a blow on the shoulder and looked into his eyes.

"That you will not do! You will not take her as your wife, friend Jemeljan."

"I shall marry her--I have resolved to do so."

"You will not marry her, for she will not go to you."

"If she does not come I will carry her off against her will."

"You can't marry her, because she has a husband."

"If she has a husband I will carry her off in company with him!"

"You can't carry her off, for she lives in a palace--she is guarded by many soldiers, and accompanied in her carriage by many outriders."

"I will take her away with her palace, her soldiers, and her carriage. I swear it by St. Gregory!"

Jelagin laughed mockingly.

"Good Jemeljan, go home and sleep out your love--that pretty woman is the Czarina!"

The hetman became pale for a moment, his breath stopped; but the next instant, with sparkling eyes, he said to Jelagin:

"In spite of this, what I have said I have said."

Jelagin showed the door to his guest. But, improbable as it may seem, Jemeljan was really not intoxicated, unless it were with the eyes of the pretty woman.

A few years elapsed. The Society of "The Nameless" was dissolved, or changed into one of another form. Katharine had her husband, the Czar, killed, and wore the crown herself. Many people said she had him killed, others took her part. It was urged that she knew what was going to happen, but could not prevent it--that she was compelled to act as she did, and to affect, after a great struggle with her generous heart, complete ignorance of poison being administered to her husband. It was said that she had acted rightly, and that the Czar's fate was a just one, for he was a wicked man; and finally, it was asserted that the whole statement was untrue, and that no one had killed Czar Peter, who died from intense inflammation of the stomach. He drank too much brandy. The immortal Voltaire is responsible for this last assertion. Whatever may have happened, Czar Peter was buried, and the Czarina Katharine now saw that her late husband belonged to those dead who do not sleep quietly. They rise--rise from their graves--stretch out their hands from their shrouds, and touch with them those who have forgotten them. They turn over in their last resting-place, and the whole earth seems to tremble under the feet of those who walk above them!

Amongst the numerous contradictory stories told, one difficult to believe, but which the people gladly credited, and which caused much bloodshed before it was wiped out of their memory, was this--that Czar Peter died neither by his own hand, nor by the hands of others, but that he still lived. It was said that a common soldier, with pock-marked face resembling the Czar, was shown in his stead to the public on the death- couch at St. Petersburg, and that the Czar himself had escaped from prison in soldier's clothes, and would return to retake his throne, to vanquish his wife, and behead his enemies! Five Czar pretenders rose one after the other in the wastes of the Russian domains. One followed the other with the motto, "Revenge on the faithless!" The usurpers conquered sometimes a northern, sometimes a southern province, collected forces, captured towns, drove out all officials, and put new ones in their places, so that it was necessary to send forces against them. If one was subjugated and driven away into the ice deserts, or captured and hung on the next tree, another Czar Peter would rise up in his place and cause rebellion, alarming the Court circle whilst they were enjoying themselves; and so things went on continually and continually. The murdered husband remained unburied, for to-day he might be put in the earth and to-morrow he would rise again, one hundred miles off, and exclaim, "I still live!" He might be killed there, but would pop out his head again from the earth, saying, "Still I live." He had a hundred lives! When five of these Peter pretenders went the way of the real Czar a sixth rose, and this one was the most dreaded and most daring of all, whose name will perpetually be inscribed in the chronicles of the Russian people as a dreadful example to all who will not be taught wisdom, and his name is Jemeljan Pugasceff! He was born as an ordinary Cossack in the Don province, and took part in the Prussian campaign, at first as a paid soldier of Prussia, later as an adherent of the Czar. At the bombardment of Bender he had become a Cossack hetman. His extraordinary physical strength, his natural common sense and inventive power, had distinguished him even at this time, but the peace which was concluded barred before him the gate of progress. He was sent with many discharged officers back to the Don. Let them go again and look after their field labors! Pugasceff's head, however, was full of other ideas than that of again commencing cheese-making, from which occupation he had been called ten years before. He hated the Czarina, and adored her! He hated the proud woman who had no right to tread upon the neck of the Russians, and he adored the beautiful woman who possessed the right to tread upon every Russian's heart! He became possessed with the mad idea that he would tear down that woman from her throne, and take her afterwards into his arms. He had his plans prepared for this. He went along the Volga, where the Roskolniks live--they who oppose the

Russian religion, and who were the adherents of the persecuted fanatics whose fathers and grandfathers had been continually extirpated by means of hanging, either on trees or scaffolds, and this only for the sole reason that they crossed themselves downwards, and not upwards, as they do in Moscow!

The Roskolniks were always ready to plot if they had any pretence and could get a leader. Pugasceff wanted to commence his scheme with these, but he was soon betrayed, and fell into the hands of the police and was carried into a Kasan prison and put into chains. He might thus go on dreaming! Pugasceff dreamed one night that he burst the iron chains from his legs, cut through the wall of the prison, jumped down from the inclosure, swam through the surrounding trench whose depth was filled with sharp spikes, and that he made his way towards the uninhabited plains of the Ural Sorodok, without a crust of bread or a decent stitch of clothing! The Jakics Cossacks are the only inhabitants of the plains of Uralszk--the most dreaded tribe in Russia--living in one of those border countries only painted in outline on the map, and a people with whom no other on the plains form acquaintanceship. They change locality from year to year. One winter a Cossack band will pay a visit to the land of the Kirghese, and burn down their wooden huts; next year a Kirgizian band will render the same service to the Cossacks! Fighting is pleasanter work in the winter. In the summer every one lives under the sky, and there are no houses to be destroyed! This people belong to the Roskolnik sect. Just a little while previously they had amused themselves by slaughtering the Russian Commissioner-General Traubenberg, with his suite, who came there to regulate how far they might be allowed to fish in the river Jaik, and with this act they thought they had clearly proved the Government had nothing to do pike! Pugasceff had just taken refuge amongst them at the time when they were dividing the arms of the Russian soldiers, and were scheming as to what they should further do. One lovely autumn night the escaped convict after a great deal of wandering in the miserable valley of Jeremina Kuriza, situated in the wildest part of the Ural Mountains, and in its yet more miserable town, Jaiczkoi, knocked at the door of the first Cossack habitation he saw and said that he was a refugee. He was received with an open heart, and got plenty of kind words and a little bread. The house-owner was himself poor; the Kirgizians had driven away his sheep. One of his sons, a priest of the Roskolnik persuasion, had been carried away from him into a lead-mine; the second had been taken to serve as a soldier, and had died; the third was hung because he had been involved in a revolt. Old Kocsenikoff remained at home without sons or family. Pugasceff listened to the grievances of his host, and said:

"These can be remedied."

"Who can raise for me my dead sons?" said the old man bitterly.

"The one who rose himself in order to kill."

"Who can that be?"

"The Czar."

"The murdered Czar?" asked the old soldier, with astonishment.

"He has been killed six times, and yet he lives. On my way here, whenever I met with people, they all asked me, 'Is it true that the Czar is not dead yet, and that he has escaped from prison?' I replied to them, 'It is true. He has found his way here, and ere long he will make his appearance before you.'"

"You say this, but how can the Czar get here?"

"He is already here."

"Where is he?"

"I am he!"

"Very well--very well," replied the old Roskolnik. "I understand what you want with me. I shall be on the spot if you wish it. All is the same to me as long as I have any one to lead me. But who will believe that you are the Czar? Hundreds and hundreds have seen him face to face. Everybody knows that the visage of the Czar was dreadfully pockmarked, whilst yours is smooth."

"We can remedy that. Has not some one lately died of black-pox in this district?"

"Every day this happens. Two days ago my last laborer died."

"Well, I shall lay in his bed, and I shall rise from it like Czar Peter."

He did what he said. He lay in the infected bed. Two days later he got the black-pox, and six weeks afterwards he rose with the same wan face as one had seen on the unfortunate Czar.

Kocsenikoff saw that a man who could play so recklessly with his life did not come here to idle away his time. This is a country where, out of ten men, nine have stored away some revenge of their own, for a future time. Amongst the first ten people to whom Kocsenikoff communicated his scheme, he found nine who were ready to assist in the daring undertaking, even at the cost of their lives; but the tenth was a traitor. He disclosed the desperate plot to Colonel Simonoff, the commander of Jaiczkoi, and the commander immediately arrested Kocsenikoff; but Pugasceff escaped on the horse which had been sent out with the Cossack who came to arrest him, and he even carried off the Cossack himself! He jumped into the saddle, patted and spurred the horse, and made his way into the forest.

History records for the benefit of future generations the name of the Cossack whom Pugasceff carried away with his horse: Csika was the name of this timid individual! This happened on September 15. Two days afterwards Pugasceff came back from the forest to the outskirts of the town Jaiczkoi. Then he had his horse, a scarlet fur-trimmed jacket, and three hundred brave horsemen. As he approached the town he had trumpets blown, and demanded that Colonel Simonoff should surrender and should come and kiss the hand of his rightful master, Czar Peter III.! Simonoff came with 5,000 horsemen and 800 Russian regular troops against the rebel, and Pugasceff was in one moment surrounded. At this instant he took a loosely sealed letter from his breast and read out his proclamation in a ringing voice to the opposing troops, in which he appealed to the faithful Cossacks of Peter III. to help him to regain his throne and to aid him to drive away usurpers, threatening with death those traitors who should oppose his command. On hearing this the Cossack troops appeared startled, and the exclamation went from mouth to month, "The Czar lives! This is the Czar!" The officers tried to quiet the soldiers, but in vain. They commenced to fight amongst themselves, and the uproar lasted till late at night, with the result that it was not Simonoff who captured Pugasceff, but the latter who captured eleven of his officers; and when he retreated from the field his three hundred men had increased to eight hundred. It was a matter of great difficulty to the Colonel to lead back the rest into the town. Pugasceff set up his camp outside in the garden of a Russian nobleman, and on his trees he hung up the eleven officers. His opponent was so much alarmed that he did not dare to attack him, but lay wait for him in the trenches, at the mouth of the cannon. Our daring friend was not quite such a lunatic as to go and meet him. He required greater success, more decisive battles, and more guns. He started against the small towns which the Government had built along the Jaik. The Roskolniks received the pseudo-Czar with wild enthusiasm. They believed that he had risen from the dead to humiliate the power of the Moscow priests, and that he intended to adopt, instead of the Court religion, that which had been persecuted. On the third day 1500 men accompanied him to battle. The stronghold of Ileczka was the first halting-place he made. It is situated about seventy versts from Jaiczkoi. He was welcomed with open gates and with acclamation, and the guard of the place went over to his side. Here he found guns and powder, and with these he was able to continue his campaign. Next followed the stronghold of Kazizna. This did not surrender of its own accord, but commenced heroically to defend itself, and Pugasceff was compelled to bombard it. In the heat of the siege the rebel Cossacks shouted out to those in the fort, and they actually turned their guns upon their own patrols. All who opposed them were strung up, and the Colonel was taken a prisoner to Pugasceff, who showed no mercy to any one who wore his hair long, which was the fashion at the time amongst the Russian officers, and for this reason the pseudo-Czar hung every officer who fell into his hands. Now, provided with guns, he made his way towards the fort of Nisnaja Osfernaja, which he also captured after a short attack. Those whom he did not kill joined him. Now he led 4,000 men, and therefore he could dare attack the stronghold of Talitseva, which was defended by two heroes, Bilof and Jelagin. The Russian authorities took up a firm position in face of the fanatical rebels, and they would have repulsed Pugasceff, if the hay stores in the fort had not been burned down. This fire gave assistance to the rebels. Bilof and Jelagin were driven out of the fort-gates, and were forced out into the plains, where they were slaughtered. When the pseudo-Czar captured the fort of Nisnaja Osfernaja, a marvelously beautiful woman came to him in the market-place and threw herself at his feet. "Mercy, my master!" The woman was very lovely, and was quite in the power of the conqueror. Her tears and excitement made her still more enchanting.

"For whom do you want pardon?"

"For my husband, who is wounded in fighting against you."

"What is the name of your husband?"

"Captain Chalof, who commanded this fort."

A noble-hearted hero no doubt would have set at liberty both husband and wife, let them be happy, and love one another. A base man would have hung the husband and kept the wife. Pugasceff killed them both! He knew very well that there were still many living who remembered that Czar Peter III. was not a man who found pleasure in women's love, and he remained true to his adopted character even in its worst extremes.

The rebels appeared to have wings. After the capture of Talicseva followed that of Csernojecsinszkaja, where the commander took flight on the approach of the rebel leader, and entrusted the defense of the fort to Captain Nilsajeff, who surrendered without firing a shot. Pugasceff, without saying "Thank you," had him hanged. He did not believe in officers who went over to the enemy. He only kept the common soldiers, and he had their hair cut short, so that in the event of their escaping he should know them again! Next morning the last stronghold in the country, Precsisztenszka, situated in the vicinity of the capital, Orenburg, surrendered to the rebels, and in the evening the mock Czar stood before the walls of Orenburg with thirty cannon and a well- equipped army! All this happened in fifteen days.

Since the moment when he carried off the Cossack who had been sent to capture him, and met Kocsenikoff, he had occupied six forts, entirely annihilated a regiment, and created another, with which he now besieged the capital of the province.

The towns of the Russian Empire are divided by great distances, and before things were decided at St. Petersburg, Marquis Pugasceff might almost have occupied half the country. It was Katharine herself who nicknamed Pugasceff Marquis, and she laughed very heartily and often in the Court circles about her extraordinary husband, who was preparing to reconquer his wife, the Czarina. The nuptial bed awaited him--it was the scaffold!

On the news of Pugasceff's approach, Reinsburg, the Governor of Orenburg, sent, under the command of Colonel Bilof, a portion of his troops to attack the rebel. Bilof started on the chase, but he shared the fate of many lion-hunters. The pursued animal ate him up, and of his entire force not one man returned to Orenburg. Instead of this, Pugasceff's forces appeared before its gates.

Reinsburg did not wish to await the bombardment, and he sent his most trusted regiment, under the command of Major Naumoff, to attack the rebels. The mock-Czar allowed it to approach the slopes of the mountains outside Orenburg, and there, with masked guns, he opened such a disastrous fire upon them that the Russians were compelled to retire to their fort utterly demoralized. Pugasceff then descended into the plains and pitched his camp before the town. The two opponents both began with the idea of tiring each other out by waiting. Pugasceff was encamped on the snow-fields. The plains of Russia are no longer green in October, and instead of tents he had huts made of branches of oak. The one force was attacked by frost--the other by starvation. Finally, starvation proved the more powerful. Naumoff sallied from the fort, and turned his attention towards occupying those heights whence his forces had been fired upon a short time previously. He succeeded in making an onslaught with his infantry upon the rebel lines, but Pugasceff, all of a sudden, changed his plan of battle, and attacked with his Cossacks the cavalry of his opponent, who took to flight. The victory fell from the grasp of Naumoff, and he was compelled to fly with his cannon, breaking his way, sword in hand, through the lines of the Cossacks. Then Pugasceff attacked in his turn. He had forty-eight guns, with which he commenced a fierce bombardment of the walls, which continued until November 9th, when he ordered his troops to storm the town. The onslaught did not succeed, for the Russians bravely defended themselves. Pugasceff, therefore, had to make up his mind to starve out his opponents. The broad plains and valleys were white with snow, the forests sparkled with icicles, as though made of silver, and during the long nights the cold reflection of the moon alone brightened the desolate wastes where the audacious dream of a daring man kept awake the spirits of his men. The dream was this: That he should be the husband of the Czarina of All the Russias.

Katharine II. was passionately fond of playing tarok, and she particularly liked that variety of the game which was later on named, after a celebrated Russian general, "Paskevics," and required four players. In addition to the Czarina, Princess Daskoff, Prince Orloff, and General Karr sat at her table. The latter was a distinguished leader of troops--in petto--and as a tarok-player without equal. He rose from the table semper victor! No one ever saw him pay, and for this reason he was a particular favorite with the Czarina. She said if she could only once succeed in winning a rouble from Karr she would have a ring welded to it and wear it suspended from her neck. It is very likely that the mistakes of his opponents aided General Karr's continual success. The two noble ladies were too much occupied with Orloff's fine eyes to be able to fix their attention wholly upon the game, whilst Orloff was so lucky in love that it would have been the greatest injustice on earth if he had been equally successful at play. Once, whilst shuffling the cards, some one casually remarked that it was a scandalous shame that an escaped Cossack like Pugasceff should be in a position to conquer a fourth of Russia in Europe, to disgrace the Russian troops time after time, to condemn the finest Russian officers to a degrading death, and now even to bombard Orenburg like a real potentate.

"I know the dandy, I know him very well," said Karr. "During the life of His Majesty I used to play cards with him at Oranienbaum. He is a stupid youngster. Whenever I called carreau, he used to give coeur."

"It appears that he plays even worse now," said the Czarina; "now he throws pique after coeur!"

It was the fashion at this time at the Russian Court to throw in every now and then a French word, and coeur in French means heart, and piquer means to sting and prick.

"Yes, because our commanders have been inactive. Were I only there!"

"Won't you have the kindness to go there?" asked Orloff mockingly.

"If Her Majesty commands me, I am ready."

"Ah! this tarok-party would suffer a too great loss in you," said Katharine, jokingly.

"Well, your Majesty might have hunting-parties at Peterhof," he said, consolingly, to the Czarina.

This was a pleasant suggestion to Katharine, for at Peterhof she had spent her brightest days, and there she had made the acquaintance of Orloff. With a smile full of grace, she nodded to General Karr.

"I don't mind, then; but in two weeks you must be back."

"Ah! what is two weeks?" returned Karr; "if your Majesty commands it, I will seat myself this very hour upon a sledge, and in three days and nights I shall be in Bugulminszka. On the fourth day I shall arrange my cards, and on the fifth I shall send word to this dandy that I am the challenger. On the sixth day I shall give 'Volat' to the rascal, and the seventh and eighth days I shall have him as Pagato ultimo, bound in chains, and bring him to your Majesty's feet!"[5]

The Czarina burst out laughing at the funny technical expressions used by the General, and entrusted Orloff to provide the celebrated Pagato- catching Gener-

5   "Volat" is an expression used in tarok to denote that no tricks have been made by an opponent. This is another term in the game, when the player announces beforehand that he will make the last trick with the Ace of Trumps.

al with every necessity. The matter was taken seriously, and Orloff promulgated the imperial ukase, according to which Karr was entrusted with the control of the South Russian troops, and at the same time he announced to him what forces he would have at his command. At Bugulminszka was General Freymann with 20,000 infantry, 2,000 cavalry, and thirty-two guns, and he would be reinforced by Colonel Csernicseff, the Governor of Szinbirszk, who had at his command 15,000 horsemen and twelve guns; while on his way he would meet Colonel Naumann with two detachments of the Body Guard. He was in particular to attach the latter to him, for they were the very flower of the army. Karr left that night. His chief tactics in campaigning consisted in speediness, but it seems that he studied this point badly, for his great predecessors, Alexander the Great, Frederick the Great, Hannibal, etc., also travelled quickly, but in company with an army, whilst Karr thought it quite sufficient if he went alone. He judged it impossible to travel faster than he did, sleighing merrily along to Bugulminszka; but it was possible. A Cossack horseman, who started the same time as he did from St. Petersburg, arrived thirty-six hours before him, informed Pugasceff of the coming of General Karr, and acquainted him as to the position of his troops. Pugasceff despatched about 2,000 Cossacks to fall upon the rear of the General, and prevent his junction with the Body Guard.

Karr did not consult any one at Bugulminszka. He pushed aside his colleague Freymann in order to be left alone to settle the affair. He said it was not a question of fighting but of chasing. He must be caught alive--this wild animal. Csernicseff was already on the way with 1,200 horsemen and twelve guns, as he had received instructions from Karr to cross the river Szakmara and prevent Pugasceff from retreating, while he himself should, with the pick of the regiment, attack him in front and thus catch him between two fires. Csernicseff thought he had to do with clever superiors, and as an ordinary divisional leader he did not dare to think his General to be so ignorant as to allow him to be attacked by the magnificent force of his opponent, nor did he think that Pugasceff would possess such want of tactics as, whilst he saw before him a strong force, to turn with all his troops to annihilate a small detachment. Both these things happened. Pugasceff quietly allowed his opponents to cross over the frozen river. Then he rushed upon them from both sides. He had the ice broken in their rear, and thus destroyed the entire force, capturing twelve guns. Csernicseff himself, with thirty-five officers, was taken prisoner, and Pugasceff had them all hanged on the trees along the roadway. Then, drunk with victory, he moved with his entire forces against Karr. He, too, was approaching hurriedly, and, thirty-six miles from Bugulminszka, the two forces met in a Cossack village. General Karr was quite astonished to find, instead of an imagined mob, a disciplined army divided into proper detachments, and provided with guns. Freymann advised him, as he had sent away the trusted squadron of Csernicseff, not to commence operations now with the cavalry, to take the village as the basis of his operations, and to use his infantry against the rebels. A series of surprises then befell Karr. He saw the despised rowdy crowd approaching with drawn sabres, he saw the coolness with which they came on in the face of the fiercest musketry fire. He saw the headlong desperation with which they rushed upon his secure position. He recognized that he had found here heroes instead of thieves. But what annoyed him most was that this rabble knew so well how to handle their cannon; for in St. Petersburg, out of precaution, Cossacks are not enlisted in the artillery, in order that no one should teach them how to serve guns. And here this ignorant people handled the guns, stolen but yesterday, as though accustomed to them all their lifetime, and their shells had already set fire to villages in many different places. The General ordered his entire line to advance with a rush, while with the reserve he sharply attacked the enemy in flank, totally defeating them. His cavalry started with drawn swords towards the fire-spurting space. Amongst the 1,500 horsemen there were only 300 Cossacks, and in the heat of battle these deserted to the enemy. Immediately General Karr saw this, he became so alarmed that he set his soldiers the example of flight. All discipline at an end, they abandoned their comrades in front, and escaped as best they could.

Pugasceff's Cossacks pursued the Russians for a distance of thirty miles, but did not succeed in overtaking the General. Fear lent him wings. Arrived at Bugulminszka, he learned that Csernicseff's horsemen had been destroyed, that the Body Guard in his own rear had been taken prisoners, and that twenty-one guns had fallen into the hands of the rebels. Upon hearing this bad news he was seized with such a bad attack of the grippe that they wrapped him up in pillows and sent him home by sledge to St. Petersburg, where the four-handed card-party awaited him, and that very night he had the misfortune to lose his XXI[6]; upon which the Czarina made the

---

6   The card next to the highest in tarok.

bon mot that Karr allowed himself twice to lose his XXI. (referring to twenty-one guns), which bon mot caused great merriment at the Russian Court.

After this victory, Pugasceff's star (if a demon may be said to possess one) attained its meridian. Perhaps it might have risen yet higher had he remained faithful to his gigantic missions, and had he not forgotten the two passions which had led him on with such astonishing rapidity-- the one being to make the Czarina his wife, the other, to crush the Russian aristocracy. Which of these two ideas was the boldest? He was only separated from their realization by a transparent film.

After Karr's defeat he had an open road to Moscow, where his appearance was awaited by 100,000 serfs burning to shake off the yoke of the aristocracy, and form a new Russian empire. Forty million helots awaited their liberator the rebel leader. Then, of a sudden, he away from him the common-sense he had possessed until now-for the sake of a pair of beautiful eyes!

After the victory of Bugulminszka a large number of envoyes from the leaders of the Baskirs appeared before him, and brought him, together with their allegiance, a pretty girl to be his wife.

The name of the maiden was Ulijanka, and she stole the heart of Pugasceff from the Czarina. At that time the adventurer believed so fully in his star that he did not behave with his usual severity. Ulijanka became his favorite, and the adventurous chief appointed Salavatke, her father, to be the ruling Prince of Baskirk. Then he commenced to surround himself with Counts and Princes. Out of the booty of plundered castles he clothed himself in magnificent Court costumes, and loaded his companions with decorations taken from the heroic Russian officers. He nominated them Generals, Colonels, Counts, and Princes. The Cossack, Csika, his first soldier, was appointed Generalissimus, and to him he entrusted half his army. He also issued roubles with his portrait under the name of Czar Peter III., and sent out a circular note with the words, "Redevivus et ultor." As he had no silver mines, he struck the roubles out of copper, of which there was plenty about. This good example was also followed by the Russians, who issued roubles to the amount of millions and millions, and made payments with them generously. Pugasceff now turned the romance of the insurrection into the parody of a reign. Instead of advancing against the unprotected cities of the Russian Empire, he attacked the defended strongholds, and, in the place of pursuing the fairy picture of his dreams which had led him thus far, he laid himself down in the mud by the side of a common woman!

Generalissimus Csika was instructed to occupy the Fort Ufa, with the troops who were entrusted to his care. The time was January, 1774, and it was so terribly cold that nothing like it had been recorded in Russian chronicles. The trees of the forest split with a noise as though a battle were proceeding, and the wild fowl fell to the ground along the roads.

To carry on a siege under such circumstances was impossible. The hardened earth would not permit the digging of trenches, and it was impossible to camp on the frozen ground.

The two rebel chiefs occupied the neighboring towns, and so cut off all supplies from the neighboring forests. In Orenburg they had already eaten up the horses belonging to the garrison, and a certain Kicskoff, the commissary, invented the idea of boiling the skins of the slaughtered animals, cutting them into small slices and mixing them with paste, which food was distributed amongst the soldiers, and gave rise to the breaking out of a scorbutic disease in the fort which rendered half the garrison incapable of work. On January the 13th, Colonel Vallenstierna tried to break his way through the rebel lines with 2,500 men, but he returned with hardly seventy. The remainder, about 2,000 men, remained on the field. At any rate, they no longer asked for food! A few hundred hussars, however, cut their way through and carried to St. Petersburg the news of what Czar Peter III. (who had now risen for the seventh time from his grave) was doing! The Czarina commenced to get tired of her adorer's conquests, so she called together her faithful generals, and asked which of them thought it possible to undertake a campaign in the depth of the Russian winter into the interior of the Russian snow deserts. This did not mean playing at war, nor a triumphal procession. It meant a battle with a furious people who, in forty years' time, would trample upon the most powerful European troops. There were four who replied that in Russia everything was possible which ought to be done. The names of these four gentlemen were: Prince Galiczin, General Bibikoff, Colonel Larionoff, and Michelson, a Swedish officer. Their number, however, was soon reduced to two at the very commencement. Larionoff returned home after the first battle of Bozal, where the rebels proved victorious, whilst Bibikoff died from the hardships of the winter campaign.

Galiczin and Michelson alone remained. The Swede had already gained fame in the Turkish campaign from his swift and daring deeds, and when he started from the Fort of Bozal against the rebels his sole troops consisted of 400 hussars and 600 infantry, with four guns. With this small force he started to the relief of the Fort of Ufa. Quickly as he proceeded, Csika's spies were quicker still, and the rebel leader was informed of the approach of the small body of the enemy. As he expected that they only intended to reinforce the garrison of Ufa, he merely sent against them 3,000 men, with nine guns, to occupy the mountain passes through which they would march on their way to Ufa. But Michelson did not go to Ufa as was expected. He seated his men on sledges, and flew along the plains to Csika's splendid camp. So unexpected, so daring, so little to be credited, was this move of his, that when he fell on Csika's vanguard at one o'clock one morning nobody opposed him. The alarmed rebels hurried headlong to the camp, and left two guns in the hands of Michelson. The Swedish hero knew well enough that the 3,000 men of the enemy who occupied the mountain pass would at once appear in answer to the sound of the guns, and that he would thus be caught between two fires; so he hastily directed his men to entrench themselves beneath their sledges in the road, and left two hundred infantry with two guns to defend them, whilst with the remaining troops he made his way towards the town of Csernakuka, whither Csika's troops had fled. Michelson saw that he had no time to lose. He placed himself at the head of his hussars, sounded the charge, and attacked the bulk of his opponents. For this they were not prepared. The bold attack caused confusion amongst them, and in a few moments the centre of the camp was cut through, and the first battery captured. He then immediately turned his attention to the two wings of the camp. After this, flight became general, and Csika's troops were dispersed like a cloud of mosquitos, leaving behind them forty-eight cannon and eight small guns. The victor now returned with his small body of troops to the sledges they had left behind, and he then entirely surrounded the 3,000 rebels. Those who were not slaughtered were captured. The victorious hero sent word to the commander of the Ufa garrison that the road was clear, and that the cannon taken from his opponents should be drawn thither. A hundred and twenty versts from Ufa he reached the flying Csika. The Generalissimus then had only forty-two officers, whilst his privates had disappeared in every direction of the wind. Michelson got hold of them all, and if he did not hang them it was only because on the six days' desert march not a single tree was to be found. In the meantime, Prince Galiczin, whose troops consisted of 6,000 men, went in pursuit of Pugasceff. On this miserable route he did not encounter the mock Czar until the beginning of March. Pugasceff waited for his opponent in the forest of Taticseva. This so-called stronghold had only wooden walls, a kind of ancient fencing. It was good enough to protect the sheep from the pillaging Baskirs, but it was not suitable for war. The genius of the rebel leader did not desert him, and he was well able to look after himself. Round the fences he dug trenches, where he piled up the snow, on which he poured water. This, after being frozen, turned almost into stone, and was, at the same time, so slippery that no one could climb over it. Here he awaited Galiczin with a portion of his troops, while the remainder occupied Orenburg. The Russian general approached the hiding-place of the mock Czar cautiously. The thick fog was of service to him, and the two opponents only perceived one another when they were standing at firing distance. A furious hand-to-hand fight ensued. The best of the rebel troops were there. Pugasceff was always in the front and where the danger was greatest, but finally the Russians climbed the ice-bulwarks, captured his guns, and drove him out of the forest. This victory cost the life of 1,000 heroic Russians, but it was a complete one! Pugasceff abandoned the field with 4,000 men and seven guns; but what was a greater loss still than his army and his guns, was that of the superstitious glamour which had surrounded him until now. The belief in his incapability of defeat, that was lost too! The revengeful Czar, who had but yesterday commenced his campaign, now had to fly to the desert, which promised him no refuge. It was only then that the real horrors of the campaign commenced. It was a war such as can be imagined in Russia only, where in the thousands and thousands of square miles of borderless desert scantily distributed hordes wander about, all hating Russian supremacy, and all born gun in hand. Pugasceff took refuge amongst these people. Once again he turned on Galiczin at Kargozki. He was again defeated, and lost his last gun. His sweetheart, Ulijanka, was also taken captive--that is, if she did not betray him! From here he escaped precipitately with his cavalry across the river Mjaes.

Here Siberia commences, and here Russia has no longer villages, but only military settlements which are divided from each other by a day's march, across plains and the ancient forests, along the ranges of the Ural Mountains--the so-called factories.

The Woszkrezenszki factory, situated one day's walk into the desert, is divided by uncut forests from the Szimszki factory, in both of which cinnamon and tin paints are made, and here are to be seen the powder factory of Usiska and the bomb factory of Szatkin, where the exiled Russian convicts work. At the meeting of the rivers are the small towns of Stepnaja, Troiczka Uszt, Magitnaja, Petroluskaja, Kojelga, guarded by native Cossacks, whilst others are garrisoned by disgraced battalions. Hither came Pugasceff with the remnants of his army. Galiczin pursued him for some time, but finally came to the conclusion that in this uninhabited country, where the solitary road is only indicated by snow- covered trenches, he could not, with his regular troops, reach an opponent whose tactics were to run away as far and as fast as possible.

Pugasceff rallied to him all the tribes along the Ural district, who deserted their homesteads and followed him.

The winter suddenly disappeared, and those mild, short April days commenced which one can only realize in Siberia, when at night the water freezes, while in the daytime the melting snow covers the expanse of waste, every mountain stream becomes a torrent, and the traveler finds in the place of every brook a vast sea. The runaway might still proceed by sledge, but the pursuer would only find before him fathomless morasses. Only one leader had the courage to pursue Pugasceff even into this land--this was Michelson. Just as the Siberian wolf who has tasted the blood of the wild boar does not swerve from the track, but pursues him even amongst reeds and morasses, so the daring leader chased his opponent from plain to plain. He never had more than 1,000 men, cavalry, artillery, and gunners, all told. Every one had to carry provisions for two weeks and 100 cartridges. The cavalry had guns as well as sabres, so that they might also fight on foot, and the artillery were supplied with axes, so that, if necessary, they might serve as carpenters, and all prepared to swim should the necessity arise. With this small force Michelson followed Pugasceff amid the horde of insurrectionary tribes, surrounded on every side by people upon whose mercy he could not count, whose language he did not understand, and whose motto was death. Yet he went amongst them in cold blood, as the sailor braves the terrors of the ocean. On the 7th of May he was attacked by the father of the pretty Ulijanka, near the Szimszki factory, with 2,000 Baskirs, who were about to join Pugasceff. Michelson dispersed them, captured their guns, and discovered from the Baskir captives that Beloborodoff, one of the dukes created by Pugasceff, was approaching with a large force of renegade Russian soldiers. Michelson caught up with them near the Jeresen stream, and drove them into the Szatkin factory. Riding all by himself, so close to them that his voice could be heard, he commenced by admonishing them to rejoin the standard of the Czarina. He was fired at more than 2,000 times from the windows of the factory, but when they saw that he was invulnerable they suddenly threw open the gates and joined his forces. From them he discovered the whereabouts of the mock Czar, who had at the time once more recovered himself, had captured three strongholds, Magitnaja, Stepnaja, and Petroluskaja, and was just then besieging Troiczka. This place he took before the arrival of Michelson, who found in lieu of a stronghold nothing but ruins, dead bodies, and Russian officers hanging from the trees. Pugasceff heard of the approach of his opponent, and, with savage cunning, laid a snare to capture the daring pursuer. He dressed his soldiers in the uniform of the dead Russian soldiers, and sent messengers to Michelson in the name of Colonel Colon that be should join him beyond Varlamora. Michelson only perceived the trick when his vanguard was attacked and two of his guns captured.

Although surrounded, he immediately fell upon the flower of Pugasceff's guard, and cut his way through just where the enemy was strongest. The net was torn asunder. It was not strong enough. Pugasceff fled before Michelson, and, with a few hundred followers, escaped into the interior of Siberia, near the lake of Arga. All of a sudden Michelson found Szalavatka at his rear with Baskir troops who had already captured the Szatkin factory, and put to the sword men, women, and children. Michelson turned back suddenly, and found the Baskir camp strongly intrenched near the river Aj. The enemy had destroyed the bridges over the river, and confidently awaited the Imperial troops. At daybreak Michelson ordered up forty horsemen and placed a rifleman behind the saddle of each, telling them to swim the river and defend themselves until the remainder of the troops joined them. His commands were carried out to the letter, amidst the most furious firing of the enemy, and the Russians gained the other side of the river without a bridge, drawing with them their cannon bound to trees. The Baskirs were dispersed and fled, but whilst Michelson was pursuing them with his cavalry, he received news that his artillery was attacked by a fresh force, and he had to return to their aid. Pugasceff himself, who again was the aggressor, stood with a regular army on the plains. The battle lasted till late at night in the forest. Finally the rebels retreated, and Michelson discovered that his opponents meant to take by surprise the Fort of Ufa. He speedily cut his way through the forest, and when Pugasceff thought himself a day's distance from his opponent, he found him face to face outside the Fort of Ufa. Michelson proved again victorious, but by this time his soldiers had not a decent piece of clothing left, nor a wearable shoe, and each man had not more than two charges. He therefore had to retreat to Ufa for fresh ammunition. It appears that Michelson was just such a dreaded opponent to Pugasceff as the man not born of a woman was to Macbeth. Immediately he disappeared from the horizon, he arose anew, and at each encounter with the pretender beat him right and left. When Michelson drove him away from Ufa, Pugasceff totally defeated the Russian leaders approaching from other directions, London, Melgunoff, Duve, and Jacubovics were swept away before him, and he burned before their very eyes the town of Birszk. With drawn sword he occupied the stronghold of Ossa, where he acquired guns, and, advancing with lightning rapidity, he stood before Kazan, which is one of the most noted towns of the province; it is the seat of an Archbishop, and there is kept the crown which the Russian Czars use at their coronation. This crown was required by the mock Czar. If he could get hold of it, and the Archbishop of Kazan would place it on his head, who could deny that he was the anointed Czar? Generals Brand and Banner had but 1,500 musketry for the defense of Kazan, but the citizens of the town took also to the guns to defend themselves from within their ancient walls. The day before the bombardment, General Potemkin, accompanied by General Larionoff, arrived at Kazan. The Imperialists had as many generals and colonels in their camp as Pugasceff had corporals who had deserted their colors, yet the horde led by the rebel stormed the stronghold of the generals. Pugasceff was the first to scale the wall, standard in hand, upon which the generals took refuge in the citadel. Larionoff fled, and on his flight to Nijni Novgorod did not once look back.

Pugasceff captured the town of Kazan, and gave it up to pillage. The Archbishop of Kazan received him before the cathedral, bestowed upon him gold to the value of half a million roubles, and promised that he would place the crown on his head immediately he procured it; it being in the citadel. Pugasceff set fire to the town in all directions, as he wanted to effect the surrender of the citadel garrison by that means. Just at this moment Michelson was on his way. The heroic General hardly allowed his troops time for rest, but again started in pursuit of Pugasceff. No news of him was heard, his footsteps alone could be traced. At Burnova he was attacked by a gang of rebels, whom he dispersed, but they were not the troops of Pugasceff. At Brajevana he came upon a detachment, but this also was not the one he was looking for. He then turned towards the Fort of Ossa, where he found a group of Baskir horsemen, whom he dispersed, capturing many others, from whom he learned that Pugasceff had crossed the river Kuma; and he knew that he would find the rebel at Kazan. He hastened after him, meeting right and left with camps and troops belonging to his adventurous opponent. He found no boats on the river Kuma, so he swam it. Two other rivers lay in his way, but neither of these prevented his progress, and when he arrived at Arksz he heard firing in the direction of Kazan. Allowing but one hour's repose to his troops, he marched through the night, and at daybreak the thick dark smoke on the horizon told him that Kazan was in flames. Pugasceff's patrols communicated to their leader that Michelson was again at hand. The mock Czar cursed upon hearing the news. Was it a devil who was again at his heels, when he believed him 300 miles off? He decided that this must not be known to the garrison, who had been forced into the citadel. He collected from his troops those whom he could spare, and stationed them in the town of Taziczin, seven miles from Kazan, to prevent the advance of the dreaded enemy. Just as he was proclaiming himself Czar Peter III. in the market-place of Taziczin, a miserable-looking woman rushed in, and fell at his feet, embracing him, and covering him with kisses. This woman was Pugasceff's wife, who thought her husband lost long ago. They had been married very young, and Pugasceff himself believed her no longer living, but the poor woman recognized him by his voice. Pugasceff did not lose his presence of mind, but, gently lifting the woman up, he said to his officers: "Look after this woman; her husband was a great friend of mine and I owe him much." But every one knew that the sham Czar was no other than the husband of Marianka, and no doubt the appearance of the peasant woman told on the spirits of the insurgent troops. The most bitter and decisive battle of the insurrection awaited them. The night divided the two armies, and it was only in the morning that Michelson could force his way into the town, whence he sent word to the people of Kazan to come to his assistance. Pugasceff again attacked him with embittered fury, and as he could not dislodge him he withdrew the remainder of his troops from Kazan and encamped on the plain. The third day of the battle, fortune turned to the side of Pugasceff. They fought for four hours, and Michelson was already surrounded, when the hero put himself at the head of his small army and made a desperate rush upon Pugasceff.

The insurrectionary forces were broken asunder. They left 3,000 men on the battlefield, and 5,000 captives fell into the hands of the victors.

Kazan was free, but the Russian Empire was not so yet.

Pugasceff, trodden a hundred times to the ground, rose once more. After his defeat at Kazan, he fled, not towards the interior of Siberia, but straight towards the heart of the Russian Empire--towards Moscow. Out of his army which was split asunder at Kazan he formed 100 battalions, and with a small number of these crossed the Volga. Immediately he appeared on the opposite banks of the river, and the entire province was enkindled: the peasantry rose in revolt against the aristocracy. Within a district of 100 miles every castle was destroyed, and one town after the other opened its gates to the mock Czar. The further he advanced the more his army increased and the faster his insurrectionary red flag travelled towards the gates of Moscow. On their way the rebels occupied forts, pillaged and destroyed the towns, and the troops which were sent against them were captured. Before the Fort of Zariczin an Imperial force challenged their advance. In the ensuing battle, every Russian officer fell, and the entire force was captured. Again Pugasceff had 25.000 men and a large number of guns, and his road would have been clear to Moscow if the ubiquitous Michelson had not been at his back! This wonderful hero did not dread his opponents, however numerous, and like the panther which drives before him the herd of buffaloes, so he drove with his small body Pugasceff's tremendous army. The rebel felt that this man had a magic power over him, and that he was in league with fate. Finally, he found a convenient place outside Sarepta, and here he awaited his opponent. It is a height which a steep mountain footpath divides, and this path is intersected by another. Pugasceff placed a portion of his best troops on the ascending path, whilst to the riff- raff he entrusted his two wings. If Michelson had caught the bull by the horns with his ordinary tactics he ought to have cut through the little footpath leading to the steep road, and if he had succeeded then, the troops which were at the point of intersection would have fallen between two fires, from which they could not have escaped. But Michelson changed his system of attack. Whilst the bombardment was going on, he, together with Colonel Melin, rushed upon the wings of the opposing forces. Pugasceff saw himself fall into the pit he had dug for others. The rebel army, terror-struck, rushed towards his camp. The forces that flew to his rescue fell at the mouth of his guns, and he had to cut his way through his own troops in order to escape from the trap. This was his last battle. He escaped with sixty men, crossed the Volga, and hid amongst the bushes of an uninhabited plain.

The Russian troops surrounded the plain whence Pugasceff and his men could not escape. And yet he still dreamt of future glory! Amidst the great desert his old ambition came back to him--he pictured the golden dome of the Kremlin, and the conquered Czarina. And with these dreams he suffered the tortures of hunger. For days and days he had no nourishment but horseflesh roasted on the reeds, which was made palatable by meadow- grass in place of salt. One night, as he was sitting over the fire and roasting his meagre dinner on a wooden spit, one of the three Cossacks who formed his body-guard said to him, "You have played your comedy long enough, Pugasceff!" The adventurer sprang up from his place.

"Slave, I am your Czar!" and whilst saying this he slew the speaker. The two others made a rush at him, struck him to the ground, bound him, tied him to a horse, and thus took him to Ural Sorodok and delivered him to General Szuvarof. It was the very same Ural Sorodok whence he had started upon his bold undertaking. From here he was taken to Moscow. The sentence passed upon him was that he should be cut up alive into small pieces. The Czarina confirmed the sentence, though her beautiful eyes had had great share of responsibility for the sinner's fate. The hangman was more merciful. It was not specified in the sentence where he should commence the work of slaughter, so he began at once with his head, and for this oversight he was sent to Siberia! Katharine about this time changed her favorite. Instead of Orloff, Potemkin, a fine fellow, was chosen.

## The Codes Of Hammurabi And Moses
## W. W. Davies

QTY

The discovery of the Hammurabi Code is one of the greatest achievements of archaeology, and is of paramount interest, not only to the student of the Bible, but also to all those interested in ancient history...

**Religion**     **ISBN:** *1-59462-338-4*     **Pages:132**
*MSRP $12.95*

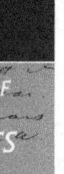

## The Theory of Moral Sentiments
## Adam Smith

QTY

This work from 1749. contains original theories of conscience amd moral judgment and it is the foundation for systemof morals.

**Philosophy**  **ISBN:** *1-59462-777-0*     **Pages:536**
*MSRP $19.95*

## Jessica's First Prayer
## Hesba Stretton

QTY

In a screened and secluded corner of one of the many railway-bridges which span the streets of London there could be seen a few years ago, from five o'clock every morning until half past eight, a tidily set-out coffee-stall, consisting of a trestle and board, upon which stood two large tin cans, with a small fire of charcoal burning under each so as to keep the coffee boiling during the early hours of the morning when the work-people were thronging into the city on their way to their daily toil...

**Childrens**   **ISBN:** *1-59462-373-2*     **Pages:84**
*MSRP $9.95*

## My Life and Work
## Henry Ford

QTY

Henry Ford revolutionized the world with his implementation of mass production for the Model T automobile. Gain valuable business insight into his life and work with his own auto-biography... "We have only started on our development of our country we have not as yet, with all our talk of wonderful progress, done more than scratch the surface. The progress has been wonderful enough but..."

**Biographies/**   **ISBN:** *1-59462-198-5*     **Pages:300**
*MSRP $21.95*

## The Art of Cross-Examination
## Francis Wellman

QTY

I presume it is the experience of every author, after his first book is published upon an important subject, to be almost overwhelmed with a wealth of ideas and illustrations which could readily have been included in his book, and which to his own mind, at least, seem to make a second edition inevitable. Such certainly was the case with me; and when the first edition had reached its sixth impression in five months, I rejoiced to learn that it seemed to my publishers that the book had met with a sufficiently favorable reception to justify a second and considerably enlarged edition. ..

**Pages:412**

Reference     ISBN: *1-59462-647-2*     *MSRP $19.95*

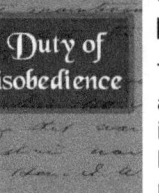

## On the Duty of Civil Disobedience
## Henry David Thoreau

QTY

Thoreau wrote his famous essay, On the Duty of Civil Disobedience, as a protest against an unjust but popular war and the immoral but popular institution of slave-owning. He did more than write—he declined to pay his taxes, and was hauled off to gaol in consequence. Who can say how much this refusal of his hastened the end of the war and of slavery ?

Law          ISBN: *1-59462-747-9*          **Pages:48**
*MSRP $7.45*

## Dream Psychology Psychoanalysis for Beginners
## Sigmund Freud

QTY

Sigmund Freud, born Sigismund Schlomo Freud (May 6, 1856 - September 23, 1939), was a Jewish-Austrian neurologist and psychiatrist who co-founded the psychoanalytic school of psychology. Freud is best known for his theories of the unconscious mind, especially involving the mechanism of repression; his redefinition of sexual desire as mobile and directed towards a wide variety of objects; and his therapeutic techniques, especially his understanding of transference in the therapeutic relationship and the presumed value of dreams as sources of insight into unconscious desires.

**Pages:196**

Dream Psychology
Psychoanalysis for Beginners

Sigmund Freud

Psychology     ISBN: *1-59462-905-6*           *MSRP $15.45*

## The Miracle of Right Thought
## Orison Swett Marden

QTY

Believe with all of your heart that you will do what you were made to do. When the mind has once formed the habit of holding cheerful, happy, prosperous pictures, it will not be easy to form the opposite habit. It does not matter how improbable or how far away this realization may see, or how dark the prospects may be, if we visualize them as best we can, as vividly as possible, hold tenaciously to them and vigorously struggle to attain them, they will gradually become actualized, realized in the life. But a desire, a longing without endeavor, a yearning abandoned or held indifferently will vanish without realization.

**Pages:360**

Self Help          ISBN: *1-59462-644-8*          *MSRP $25.45*

**The Rosicrucian Cosmo-Conception Mystic Christianity** *by Max Heindel*    ISBN: *1-59462-188-8*   **$38.95**
*The Rosicrucian Cosmo-conception is not dogmatic, neither does it appeal to any other authority than the reason of the student. It is: not controversial, but is: sent forth in the, hope that it may help to clear...*    New Age/Religion Pages 646

**Abandonment To Divine Providence** *by Jean-Pierre de Caussade*    ISBN: *1-59462-228-0*   **$25.95**
*"The Rev. Jean Pierre de Caussade was one of the most remarkable spiritual writers in France in the 18th Century. His death took place at Toulouse in 1751. His works have gone through many editions and have been republished...*    Inspirational/Religion Pages 400

**Mental Chemistry** *by Charles Haanel*    ISBN: *1-59462-192-6*   **$23.95**
*Mental Chemistry allows the change of material conditions by combining and appropriately utilizing the power of the mind. Much like applied chemistry creates something new and unique out of careful combinations of chemicals the mastery of mental chemistry...*    New Age/Business Pages 354

**The Letters of Robert Browning and Elizabeth Barret Barrett 1845-1846 vol II**    ISBN: *1-59462-193-4*   **$35.95**
*by Robert Browning and Elizabeth Barrett*    Biographies Pages 596

**Gleanings In Genesis (volume I)** *by Arthur W. Pink*    ISBN: *1-59462-130-6*   **$27.45**
*Appropriately has Genesis been termed "the seed plot of the Bible" for in it we have, in germ form, almost all of the great doctrines which are afterwards fully developed in the books of Scripture which follow...*    Religion/Inspirational Pages 420

**The Master Key** *by L. W. de Laurence*    ISBN: *1-59462-001-6*   **$30.95**
*In no branch of human knowledge has there been a more lively increase of the spirit of research during the past few years than in the study of Psychology, Concentration and Mental Discipline. The requests for authentic lessons in Thought Control, Mental Discipline and...*    New Age/Business Pages 422

**The Lesser Key Of Solomon Goetia** *by L. W. de Laurence*    ISBN: *1-59462-092-X*   **$9.95**
*This translation of the first book of the "Lernegton" which is now for the first time made accessible to students of Talismanic Magic was done, after careful collation and edition, from numerous Ancient Manuscripts in Hebrew, Latin, and French...*    New Age/Occult Pages 92

**Rubaiyat Of Omar Khayyam** *by Edward Fitzgerald*    ISBN:*1-59462-332-5*   **$13.95**
*Edward Fitzgerald, whom the world has already learned, in spite of his own efforts to remain within the shadow of anonymity, to look upon as one of the rarest poets of the century, was born at Bredfield, in Suffolk, on the 31st of March, 1809. He was the third son of John Purcell...*    Music Pages 172

**Ancient Law** *by Henry Maine*    ISBN: *1-59462-128-4*   **$29.95**
*The chief object of the following pages is to indicate some of the earliest ideas of mankind, as they are reflected in Ancient Law, and to point out the relation of those ideas to modern thought.*    Religion/History Pages 452

**Far-Away Stories** *by William J. Locke*    ISBN: *1-59462-129-2*   **$19.45**
*"Good wine needs no bush, but a collection of mixed vintages does. And this book is just such a collection. Some of the stories I do not want to remain buried for ever in the museum files of dead magazine-numbers an author's not unpardonable vanity..."*    Fiction Pages 272

**Life of David Crockett** *by David Crockett*    ISBN: *1-59462-250-7*   **$27.45**
*"Colonel David Crockett was one of the most remarkable men of the times in which he lived. Born in humble life, but gifted with a strong will, an indomitable courage, and unremitting perseverance...*    Biographies/New Age Pages 424

**Lip-Reading** *by Edward Nitchie*    ISBN: *1-59462-206-X*   **$25.95**
*Edward B. Nitchie, founder of the New York School for the Hard of Hearing, now the Nitchie School of Lip-Reading, Inc, wrote "LIP-READING Principles and Practice". The development and perfecting of this meritorious work on lip-reading was an undertaking...*    How-to Pages 400

**A Handbook of Suggestive Therapeutics, Applied Hypnotism, Psychic Science**    ISBN: *1-59462-214-0*   **$24.95**
*by Henry Munro*    Health/New Age/Health/Self-help Pages 376

**A Doll's House: and Two Other Plays** *by Henrik Ibsen*    ISBN: *1-59462-112-8*   **$19.95**
*Henrik Ibsen created this classic when in revolutionary 1848 Rome. Introducing some striking concepts in playwriting for the realist genre, this play has been studied the world over.*    Fiction/Classics/Plays 308

**The Light of Asia** *by sir Edwin Arnold*    ISBN: *1-59462-204-3*   **$13.95**
*In this poetic masterpiece, Edwin Arnold describes the life and teachings of Buddha. The man who was to become known as Buddha to the world was born as Prince Gautama of India but he rejected the worldly riches and abandoned the reigns of power when...*    Religion/History/Biographies Pages 170

**The Complete Works of Guy de Maupassant** *by Guy de Maupassant*    ISBN: *1-59462-157-8*   **$16.95**
*"For days and days, nights and nights, I had dreamed of that first kiss which was to consecrate our engagement, and I knew not on what spot I should put my lips..."*    Fiction/Classics Pages 240

**The Art of Cross-Examination** *by Francis L. Wellman*    ISBN: *1-59462-309-0*   **$26.95**
*Written by a renowned trial lawyer, Wellman imparts his experience and uses case studies to explain how to use psychology to extract desired information through questioning.*    How-to/Science/Reference Pages 408

**Answered or Unanswered?** *by Louisa Vaughan*    ISBN: *1-59462-248-5*   **$10.95**
*Miracles of Faith in China*    Religion Pages 112

**The Edinburgh Lectures on Mental Science (1909)** *by Thomas*    ISBN: *1-59462-008-3*   **$11.95**
*This book contains the substance of a course of lectures recently given by the writer in the Queen Street Hall, Edinburgh. Its purpose is to indicate the Natural Principles governing the relation between Mental Action and Material Conditions...*    New Age/Psychology Pages 148

**Ayesha** *by H. Rider Haggard*    ISBN: *1-59462-301-5*   **$24.95**
*Verily and indeed it is the unexpected that happens! Probably if there was one person upon the earth from whom the Editor of this, and of a certain previous history, did not expect to hear again...*    Classics Pages 380

**Ayala's Angel** *by Anthony Trollope*    ISBN: *1-59462-352-X*   **$29.95**
*The two girls were both pretty, but Lucy who was twenty-one who supposed to be simple and comparatively unattractive, whereas Ayala was credited, as her Bombwhat romantic name might show, with poetic charm and a taste for romance, Ayala when her father died was nineteen...*    Fiction Pages 484

**The American Commonwealth** *by James Bryce*    ISBN: *1-59462-286-8*   **$34.45**
*An interpretation of American democratic political theory. It examines political mechanics and society from the perspective of Scotsman James Bryce*    Politics Pages 572

**Stories of the Pilgrims** *by Margaret P. Pumphrey*    ISBN: *1-59462-116-0*   **$17.95**
*This book explores pilgrims religious oppression in England as well as their escape to Holland and eventual crossing to America on the Mayflower, and their early days in New England...*    History Pages 268

**QTY**

**The Fasting Cure** *by Sinclair Upton*      **ISBN:** *1-59462-222-1*   **$13.95**
*In the Cosmopolitan Magazine for May, 1910, and in the Contemporary Review (London) for April, 1910, I published an article dealing with my experiences in fasting. I have written a great many magazine articles, but never one which attracted so much attention...* New Age/Self Help/Health Pages 164

**Hebrew Astrology** *by Sepharial*      **ISBN:** *1-59462-308-2*   **$13.45**
*In these days of advanced thinking it is a matter of common observation that we have left many of the old landmarks behind and that we are now pressing forward to greater heights and to a wider horizon than that which represented the mind-content of our progenitors...* Astrology Pages 144

**Thought Vibration or The Law of Attraction in the Thought World**      **ISBN:** *1-59462-127-6*   **$12.95**
*by William Walker Atkinson* Psychology/Religion Pages 144

**Optimism** *by Helen Keller*      **ISBN:** *1-59462-108-X*   **$15.95**
*Helen Keller was blind, deaf, and mute since 19 months old, yet famously learned how to overcome these handicaps, communicate with the world, and spread her lectures promoting optimism. An inspiring read for everyone...* Biographies/Inspirational Pages 84

**Sara Crewe** *by Frances Burnett*      **ISBN:** *1-59462-360-0*   **$9.45**
*In the first place, Miss Minchin lived in London. Her home was a large, dull, tall one, in a large, dull square, where all the houses were alike, and all the sparrows were alike, and where all the door-knockers made the same heavy sound...* Childrens/Classic Pages 88

**The Autobiography of Benjamin Franklin** *by Benjamin Franklin*      **ISBN:** *1-59462-135-7*   **$24.95**
*The Autobiography of Benjamin Franklin has probably been more extensively read than any other American historical work, and no other book of its kind has had such ups and downs of fortune. Franklin lived for many years in England, where he was agent...* Biographies/History Pages 332

| Name | |
|---|---|
| Email | |
| Telephone | |
| Address | |
| | |
| City, State ZIP | |

☐ **Credit Card**        ☐ **Check / Money Order**

| Credit Card Number | |
|---|---|
| Expiration Date | |
| Signature | |

Please Mail to:   Book Jungle
PO Box 2226
Champaign, IL 61825
or Fax to:       630-214-0564

## ORDERING INFORMATION

**web**: *www.bookjungle.com*
**email**: *sales@bookjungle.com*
**fax**: *630-214-0564*
**mail**: *Book Jungle PO Box 2226 Champaign, IL 61825*
**or PayPal** *to sales@bookjungle.com*

*Please contact us for bulk discounts*

## DIRECT-ORDER TERMS

**20% Discount if You Order
Two or More Books**
Free Domestic Shipping!
Accepted: Master Card, Visa,
Discover, American Express